A CHRISTIAN'S POCKET GUIDE TO

LOVING
THE OLD TESTAMENT

A Christian's Pocket Guide to Loving the Old Testament, and *Alec Motyer's recent volume* Preaching? *prove that faithful believers 'will still bear fruit in old age–they will stay fresh and green.' (Ps. 92:14) Why? Because they will continue 'proclaiming, "The Lord is upright; he is my Rock, and there is no wickedness in him."' (Ps. 92:15)*

Tim Keller
Senior Pastor,
Redeemer Presbyterian Church, New York City, New York

...If the world is still here in a hundred years' time, these thrilling pages will still be looked upon as a treasure trove among God's faithful people.

Richard Bewes
Rector Emeritus,
All Souls Church, Langham Place, London

...it is a huge privilege to commend the author of the Pocket Guide you now hold in your hand – although, quite frankly, his work speaks for itself so well that it does not need me to approve it.

D.A.Carson
Research Professor of New Testament,
Trinity Evangelical Divinity School, Deerfield, Illinois

Now 90, Alec Motyer retains all his old clarity, warmth and charm as he shares his infectious affection for, and insight into, Jesus's Bible. This is a first-rate get-you-started book.

J.I. Packer
Board of Governors' Professor of Theology,
Regent College, Vancouver, Canada

A CHRISTIAN'S POCKET GUIDE TO

LOVING
THE OLD TESTAMENT

ALEC MOTYER

To

Brian Ruff
Alasdair Paine
Nick Hiscocks

My successors (to my delight) in ministry at Christ
Church Westbourne, Bournemouth

Copyright © Alec Motyer 2015

paperback ISBN 978-1-78191-580-6
epub ISBN 978-1-78191-612-4
Mobi ISBN 978-1-78191-613-1

Published in 2015
by
Christian Focus Publications Ltd,
Geanies House, Fearn, Ross-shire,
IV20 1TW, Scotland, Great Britain
www.christianfocus.com

Cover design by Daniel van Straaten
Printed by Norhaven, Denmark

CONTENTS

⚠ Warning
🖉 Don't Forget
⑦ Stop and Think
⁎ Point of Interest

FOREWORD

Tim Keller

Approximately forty years ago, during the summer between my undergraduate college years and seminary, I was working and living with my parents in Johnstown, Pennsylvania. One evening I drove over the mountains down into a long valley in the midst of the Laurel Highlands and came eventually to the Ligonier Valley Study Center, just outside the little Western Pennsylvania hamlet of Stahlstown, where R.C. Sproul was hosting at his regular weekly Question and Answer session a British Old Testament scholar, J. Alec Motyer. As a still fairly new Christian, I found the Old Testament to be a confusing and off-putting part of the Bible.

I will always remember his answer to a question about the relationship of Old Testament Israel to the church

(I can't remember if R.C. posed it to him or someone from the audience). After saying something about the discontinuities, he insisted that we were all one people of God. Then he asked us to imagine how the Israelites under Moses would have given their 'testimony' to someone who asked for it. They would have said something like this:

> We were in a foreign land, in bondage, under the sentence of death. But our mediator—the one who stands between us and God—came to us with the promise of deliverance. We trusted in the promises of God, took shelter under the blood of the lamb, and he led us out. Now we are on the way to the Promised Land. We are not there yet, of course, but we have the law to guide us, and through blood sacrifice we also have his presence in our midst. So he will stay with us until we get to our true country, our everlasting home.

Then Dr Motyer concluded: 'Now think about it. A Christian today could say the same thing, almost word for word.'

My young self was thunderstruck. I had held the vague, unexamined impression that in the Old Testament people were saved through obeying a host of detailed laws but that today we were freely forgiven and accepted by faith. This little thought experiment showed me, in a stroke, not only that the Israelites had been saved by grace and that God's salvation had been by costly atonement and grace all along, but also that the pursuit of holiness, pilgrimage, obedience, and deep community should characterize Christians as well.

Not long after this I heard a series of lectures by Edmund P. Clowney on the importance of ministers always preaching Christ, even when they are preaching from the Old Testament. Dr Motyer's little bombshell and Ed Clowney's lectures started me on a lifetime quest to preach Christ and the gospel every time I expound a Biblical text. They are, in a sense, the fathers of my preaching ministry.

While I believe I have read and used all of Dr Motyer's published works over the course of my life, three of his books were transformative to my ministry in particular. In my early days as a preacher his commentary on Amos, sub-titled 'The Day of the Lion', was a huge help to me as I struggled for the first time to expound the minor prophets. That work showed me God's emphasis on social justice and righteousness, a standard he applied not only to his own covenant people but also to the nations around them.

The second intervention came a couple of decades later, when I was convicted about the shallowness of my prayer life. In response, I began to dig into the Psalms, and the two resources I relied on were Derek Kidner's Tyndale commentary and Alec Motyer's brief but luminous treatment of the Psalms in the *New Bible Commentary: 21st Century Edition*. Dr Motyer's compact description of the psalmists—that they were people who knew far less about God than we do, yet loved him a great deal more—is a crucial guide for interpreting the anguished cries, shouts of praise, and declarations of love we meet in God's own Prayer Book. It is clear at some points that we are reading authors who were writing about God's salvation before the 'fullness of time' had come and the

Cross laid bare God's plan for saving the world. And yet the psalmists—with their less granular understanding of the outworkings of it all—did indeed grasp the gospel of salvation by grace, substitutionary atonement, and faith. Across the 150 psalms we see virtually every human condition and emotion set before God and transfigured by prayer. The authors' love for God convicts, uplifts, and instructs us as nothing else can. Through Motyer and Kidner I was ushered into a new stage in my journey toward fellowship with God.

Finally, a few years ago I tackled a series of sermons expounding the book of Exodus mainly because I saw that Dr Motyer had produced *The Message of Exodus* in 2005. It did not disappoint and became my main go-to resource for the series.

This book, *A Christian's Pocket Guide to Loving the Old Testament*, and his recent volume *Preaching? Simple Teaching on Simply Preaching* prove that faithful believers 'will still bear fruit in old age—they will stay fresh and green.' (Ps. 92:14) Why? Because they will continue 'proclaiming, "The Lord is upright; he is my Rock, and there is no wickedness in him."' (Ps. 92:15)

Tim Keller,
Redeemer Presbyterian Church
New York City
August, 2014

PREFACE

The title of this small book expresses exactly where I am today, nearly nine decades since my grandmother introduced me to the wonderful stories of the Old Testament. The love of the Bible, not least the Old Testament, which she shared with me has been the 'story line' of my life. Privilege and delight, therefore, came together when I was asked to offer three lectures under the title 'Loving the Old Testament' at 'The Bible by the Beach' conference in 2012 AD.

Those lectures have now been given a new lease of life in this book.

1. Everything has, of course, been re-written. It is only in the case of very rare and exceptional speakers that the spoken word can be transferred,

without alteration, to paper. The two forms of communication—speech and writing—demand different treatment. What can be sketched out in a lecture needs to be spelled out on paper; the speaker's repetitions, so necessary in order to give hearers time to listen, are tedious in print. Likewise, most illustrations, even if effective in a sermon, are rarely more than banal when written down. Everything has to be filtered through a different lens for the new medium.

2. The three lectures have now become fourteen chapters—for two reasons: first, in the hope of making the material more easily digestible in distinct 'bites'; and secondly, because the exercise of writing exposed the need to introduce topics that did not feature in the lectures at all, or to expand some that did.

I have enjoyed the work of re-presenting the lectures, and I hope you will enjoy reading the result. Long ago we used to sing, in what I fear may be a by-gone hymn: 'Teach me to love your sacred Word, and view my Saviour there.' It applies equally to the Old Testament as to the New; it is my prayer for myself day by day: it is my prayer for you as you read my book.

Alec Motyer

1

BEGIN HERE!

The Bible is God's gift to us as a domestic and personal 'means of grace'. Just as the Lord's Supper is a corporate 'means of grace' at which the Lord ministers to his believing children his promises of eternal salvation, and assures us of our 'interest' in them, so, day by day, in the family and in the privacy of personal times of devotion, we open his holy Word, hear his voice, learn his truth, delight in his presence, embrace his promises, and re-commit ourselves to the life of the obedience of faith.

It is a particularly lovely thing to take up an attitude of prayer as we hear the Word of God so that we can move straight from the Scriptures to talk to our Heavenly

Father, to the Lord Jesus, and to the Holy Spirit, bringing before him the truth he has just imparted, turning it to prayer, praise, adoration, thanksgiving and intercession.

So will you take up an attitude of readiness for prayer as you read the Word of God as it is written in Psalm 19, a Psalm of David. The Word of God says;

> The law of the Lord is perfect, restoring the soul. The testimony of the Lord is reliable, making wise the simple. The precepts of the Lord are right, rejoicing the heart. The commandment of the Lord is pure, enlightening the eyes. The fear of the Lord is clean, enduring forever. The judgements of the Lord are true; they are righteous altogether. More to be desired are they than gold, yea, than much fine gold; sweeter also than honey and the honeycomb (Ps. 19:7–11).

Lovely words in Psalm 19, are they not? We could go on reading them over and over again and pondering them. Delightful words! But just look at verse 10 again. That will do for now. 'More to be desired are they than gold, yea, than much fine gold; sweeter also than honey, honey flowing from the comb.'

INTRINSIC RICHES; EXPERIENCED DELIGHT

'More to be desired than gold'—that's the intrinsic value of the Word of God. Intrinsic—the value that is there; the value that inheres in the Word of God—gold and fine gold in abundance. You know that the Psalms have come to us in Hebrew. If we were to open up the translation of verse 10 just a fraction—not paraphrasing but opening up the meaning that is there, we'd say 'More to be desired than gold, yes, and deservedly so.' This is the intrinsic value of the Word of God.

But then alongside the intrinsic value there is the experienced value—'sweeter than honey and the honeycomb.' Do you like honey? The experienced value of the Word of God—honey flowing out of the honeycomb for our delectation and enjoyment, tasting the sweetness of it on our tongues and palates. What a beautiful description of the Word of God, and, please God, one well known to you and me in personal experience, when the pure gold God has infused into his Word becomes the pure honey of our delight! Very often it may be an old truth, already well known but suddenly alive with fresh vigour and tastiness; it may be a new truth or a new emphasis but in it and with it the fresh honey is flowing from the comb.

THE GOLDMINE; THE HONEYCOMB

Now do something very obvious, tell yourself where this verse is in the Bible—Psalm 19, yes, and where, pray, is Psalm 19? It's not part of the Book of Revelation, looking back over the whole book of Scripture. It's not part of what we call the New Testament, where the presence of our Lord Jesus Christ would lead us to expect the finest gold and the purest honey. It's bang in the middle of what we call the Old Testament, and it says about the Old Testament that it has greater intrinsic value than much fine gold and greater sweetness in experience than fresh honey flowing out of the honeycomb. And I say for myself, 'Lord, make your Word like that to me. And particularly this larger bit of our Bibles, the bit at the beginning that we call the Old Testament—make it to me the purest of gold, the sweetest of honey.

Some Old Testament references to the Word of God:

Read Ezekiel 2:8–3:4 and note how this 'illustrative experience' underlines (1) the completeness of God's Word as given, 2:10a, written on both sides, leaving no room for addition; (2) the clarity of its contents, 2:10b, pointing to the ability of the word to make itself plain to the reader; (3) Its inherent nourishment, 2:8; 3:1, 3a; (4) how 'palatable' it is to those who feed on it, 3:3b; cf. Jer. 15:16; (5) Its effectiveness as a 'tool' for ministry, 3:4— NB (NKJV) 'with', i.e., 'by means of'. The Word is the

Seven titles for the Word of God from Psalm 1 (NKJV):

'**law**' = 'teaching', the word to instruct (v. 1);

'**testimonies**', what God 'testifies to' as his truth and the truth about himself, the word to reveal (v. 2);

'**ways**', the word as the guide to characteristic life-style (v. 3);

'**precepts**', the word as instruction for the details of daily life (v. 4);

'**statutes**', from the verb 'to engrave', the word in its permanency, engraven in the rock (v. 5);

'**commandments**', the word given by God for our obedience (v. 6);

'**judgments**'—as of the authoritative pronouncements of a judge; the word expressing what the Lord himself has 'decided upon' as truth to hold and life to live (v. 7).

only weapon given to Ezekiel to deal with the inveterate hard-heartedness of his audience (2:7).

Genesis 1:3, 6–7, etc. refer to the Word in Creation, to its creative power and control (cf. Ps. 33:6; 147:15; 148:5).

Isaiah 40:6–8 speaks of the enduring Word.

The psalmist extols its purity (Ps. 12:6); it demands purity in those who would use it (Jer. 15:19).

2

THE THREEFOLD BOOK

What, then, is in this book which we have inherited as 'The Old Testament'?

The order in which we have the books of the Old Testament in our English Bibles has come to us through a third century BC Greek translation of the Hebrew Bible. Why they changed the order is only known to them! The Hebrew Bible, however, has come to us as the 'threefold book'—the Law, the Prophets, and the Writings.

'The Law' is the title of the first five books, Genesis to Deuteronomy: The Law of Moses.

'The Prophets' falls into two parts. 'The Former Prophets', Joshua, Judges, Samuel, Kings; and 'the Latter

Prophets'. i.e., the 'major prophets' Isaiah, Jeremiah, Ezekiel; and the 'minor' prophets : Hosea, Joel, Amos, Obadiah, Jonah, Micah, Nahum, Habakkuk Zephaniah. Haggai, Zechariah, Malachi.

'The Writings': Psalms, Proverbs, Job, Song of Solomon, Ruth, Lamentations, Ecclesiastes, Esther, Daniel, Ezra, Nehemiah, Chronicles.

THE BIBLE AS JESUS KNEW IT?

The way the Hebrew Bible is set out requires some comments and explanations. We start by noting its three-fold shape, and recall at once how Jesus, on the evening of his resurrection, 'opened their understanding that they might comprehend the Scriptures,' and, in particular, he instructed them that 'all things must be fulfilled which were written in the Law of Moses and the Prophets and the Psalms' concerning himself (Luke 24:44–5). There, in summary, is the threefold book, the third section being entitled by its first and largest component, 'The Psalms'. The same feature occurs in Mark 1:2 (cf., NIV) where the whole collection of the Prophets is entitled 'Isaiah the prophet', its first book. Another indication that Jesus' Bible was our Old Testament is found in Matthew 23:35 where our Lord reviews the whole history of rejection of the Word of God from the blood of righteous Abel to the blood of Zechariah, that is from the first (Gen. 4:8) to the last (2 Chron. 24:21) books of the Bible as he knew it. What a stimulus to loving the Old Testament! It is his Bible, and our devotion to it is part of our longing to be like him.

WHAT IS A PROPHET?

A second issue raised by the Hebrew classification of Old Testament books is the fact that it calls what we think of as history books (Joshua, Judges, Samuel, Kings) as 'prophets'. How can history be prophecy?

Starting at the beginning, we first ask what a prophet is. At the end of Exodus 6 and the beginning of Exodus 7 the word 'prophet' is used in what is otherwise a wholly secular situation—and it provides us with a perfect illustration of its meaning. Moses was initially aware of being unequipped for the task the Lord assigned to him: 'I am of uncircumcised lips, and how shall Pharaoh heed me?' (6:29). His lips, he felt, had never been touched by divine grace, and on a simply natural level he was ungifted as a speaker. The Lord's solution was to conscript Moses' brother Aaron onto the team. Moses would instruct Aaron what to say; Aaron would do the speaking. But the Lord did not put it like that. He said: 'I have made you as God to Pharaoh, and Aaron…shall be your prophet' (7:1). The sequence is clear: God speaks the word to the prophet; the prophet carries the word to the audience. 'You shall speak all that I command you. And Aaron… shall speak to Pharaoh' (7:2).

This is the ground rule of prophecy, whether for Moses, the archetypal prophet (Deut. 34:10), or for any of the prophets, named or unnamed, who followed in his train. It is not that God found himself admiring what someone was saying, and decided to add an ingredient called 'inspiration' to it. No, the word originated in God, and was shared with the prophet to pass it on. This, indeed, is why the prophets were able to introduce their ministry by saying 'Thus says the Lord'—or, more literally, 'This is what the Lord has said.' They meant it very literally: if the Lord had chosen to come and speak in his own person instead of sending me, this is, word for word, what he would have said.

'THE WORD OF THE LORD CAME'

We are dealing here, of course, with a miracle and a mystery. The miracle is that though the prophet was saying exactly what the Lord wanted said, he was also speaking in his own human person, using the vocabulary, idioms, figures of speech, literary style that was naturally his. So, for example, Jeremiah can begin his book 'The words of Jeremiah…to whom the word of the Lord came' (1:1,2). Or Amos: 'The words of Amos…Thus says the Lord' (1:1,3). This claim equally to human individuality and divine inspiration can be seen worked out in each of the books of the prophets. The more we enter into what they wrote (even in English translation) the more we see how each prophet is using his own words and style, and imparting his individual 'feel' to his book, whether the 'Miltonic', 'Beethovenesque' Hebrew of Isaiah, or the more 'chatty' style of Malachi.

Throughout, the mystery of inspiration remains un-explained. At the start of his book Jeremiah says three times (1:2,3,4) that the word of the Lord 'came', but 'came' does not here translate a verb of motion; it represents the verb 'to be'—'the word of the Lord was', or, more in keeping with the force of the verb 'to be' in Hebrew, 'the word of the Lord became a living reality to.'

We would like to know a great deal more about this key topic, but the Bible remains silent. It insists on the fact, but conceals the mechanism. Illustrations are possible; explanations are impossible. The simplest (and, I believe, the most effective) illustration is a stained glass window. Outside the window there is (for the purposes of the illustration) the pure sunlight; inside, that pure light is broken up into the colours and patterns introduced by the stained glass. Yet the light and the colorations are not at variance; each coloured panel or shard of glass is there by the design of the craftsman, and the fresh colours, the story, now imposed on the pure sunlight does not distort it, but enables it to be what the craftsman intended. Exactly so, the prophets were prepared individuals (Jer. 1:5), who, by doing what came naturally to them, were by that very fact, enabled to convey without distortion the word and truth of God.

HISTORY, HIS STORY

We will return to this topic later, so little need be said here. The task of the prophet is to convey God's revealed truth. Bible historians did this by so writing history as to reveal the hand, the principles and the working of God as sovereign in the affairs of the world (Dan. 4:17b). This does not mean that they distorted or invented facts to make them fit a theological preconception. Certainly not! Every historian reveals his historian's skill in the judicious choice he makes from the multiplicity of facts and events that are available to him. His written history is a selection made in the interests of what he thinks important. We read Bible history to learn of God.

? Think of the way Matthew, Mark and Luke largely draw on the same material yet present their distinct portraits of the Lord Jesus. John lets us know how selective the Gospel Writers (John 21:25) had to be, yet selection did not distort their history. In exactly the same way Old Testament historians were selective in their choice of facts, and accurate in their portrayal both of the course of history and of the God whose story history is.

3

JESUS AND THE NOT-SO-SILLY QUESTION

Let me ask a silly question. They say if you ask a silly question, you get a silly answer, but in this case we're going to ask a seemingly silly question but get a most important answer.

My silly question is this—is there such a thing as the Old Testament?

'Yes, of course there is'—you might well reply—'it's the first and much larger bit of our Bibles.' In fact it is about three-quarters of the whole, so, yes, it is unmistakeably there. It's also the odd bit. It's full of good stories, and many of them (especially if you are like me in the prime of life!), you read in Sunday School and you learned them, and savoured them—really good stories, but then you grew up and you said, 'Ah, but there are too many wars in that bit of the Bible, and it's full of strange ceremonies that are beyond understanding, and lists of regulations it's hard to identify with.' Yes, that bit of the Bible, and yes, it does exist, doesn't it?

WHAT WOULD JESUS SAY?

But that's not quite what my question means. I'm not talking about the fact that there are these pages in our Bible. I still ask my questions, 'Does the Old Testament exist?' And 'Is there such a thing as the Old Testament?', but I want to put them to their proper test. Suppose we went to the Lord Jesus Christ and said to him, 'Please tell me why do you keep quoting from the Old Testament?' He would say, 'The old what? I don't know what you mean. What do you mean the "Old Testament?"' And in our poor flustered way, because we didn't expect that answer, we would begin to try to explain what we meant by our question, 'Why do you keep quoting from the Old Testament?' And in the long run, the Lord Jesus would say to us, 'Oh, I see! You mean the Holy Scriptures. Why ever do you call them by such an odd name? You mean the Scriptures,' as we find it in John 10:35—'The Scripture cannot be broken.' That is the wording he would have used: not 'the Old Testament' but 'the Scripture'. And if we went on talking to our precious Saviour, He would say again, 'Oh now I see what you mean! You mean 'the Word of God'—just as we hear his words in Mark 7:13,

'Making the Word of God of none effect because of your tradition'. And if we pursued the matter a little further then He would say, 'Why do you call it the Old Testament? It is God's Law. It is "the Law": Luke 10:26—'What is written in the Law? What is your reading of it?'

THE SCRIPTURES, THE WORD, THE LAW

Jesus would not have known what we meant by 'the Old Testament'. He would have said, 'The Scriptures', 'the Word of God', 'the Law'. As to their form—the Scriptures—they come to us in written form; as to their nature and authority, they are 'the Word of God'. The prophets in the Old Testament were apt to introduce their sermons by saying, 'Thus says the Lord' (more literally, 'This is what the Lord has said') and (as we have noted) what they meant is this, that 'if the Lord God Almighty had chosen to come and talk to you in His own Person instead of sending me, the prophet, to do it, this is exactly word for word what He would have said.' It is 'the Word of God'—divine in its ultimate origin and therefore prized and authoritative to us as what our God has spoken and speaks to us.

Finally, as to its content, it is 'the Law'. We must be very careful over that word because in our common use it means regulations, prescriptions, bits and bobs to be obeyed. 'Law' suggests a narrow focus on rules, legislation, even on restrictions and prohibitions, but, in the Bible, 'law' means 'teaching'. It has its regulatory, legalistic component, but basically it means an imparting of the truth that the Lord wishes to share with His people. Proverbs 4:1–2 is a good illustration: 'Hear, my children (lit., sons), the instruction of a father...Do not forsake my law.' Do you see the attractive picture sketched here?—a loving and concerned father teaching his dear sons in readiness for life. Sometimes the Lord teaches us in his word by direct statement of the truth, and sometimes He teaches by giving us rules to obey; very often He teaches us through events and experiences, or, in the Psalms, by the experience of others as they meditate on the changes and chances of life. But his 'law' is always His teaching, 'the law of God'. In Luke 10:26 the Lord Jesus Christ looks back over the whole sweep of what we call The Old Testament and, by calling it 'the law', says, in effect, 'That is God's teaching.'

So is there such a thing as The Old Testament? Well, yes and no. Yes, because it's there in our Bibles. Yes, because we have inherited this strange description, 'the Old Testament', and we are too late to get rid of it. No, because the time-honoured title does not really describe what we have. We take our stand alongside the Lord Jesus Christ, and what we have is, (1) The written form—the Scriptures. (2) The authoritative, inspired content—the Word of God. (3) Divine teaching for our instruction and direction.

PAUL'S PERSPECTIVE

Paul sees the whole Bible as the Word of God: (1) He reminds Timothy of what he has inherited, '...from childhood (lit., infancy) you have known the holy Scriptures (lit, sacred writings)' (2 Tim. 3:15), what we call 'the Old Testament'. But (2) he has already pointed Timothy to what he now possesses in principle, 'you have carefully followed my doctrine…continue in the things which you have learned…knowing from whom you have learned them' (2 Tim. 3:10, 14) Paul is referring, of course, to his own inspired writings, but his words cover in principle the apostolic scriptures of the New Testament. Then (3), bringing Old and New together, he teaches that 'all scripture is given by inspiration of God, and is profitable for doctrine (teaching the truth), for reproof (correcting errors in thought and conduct), for correction (redirecting the course of life), for instruction in righteousness (educating the believer—from infancy, v. 14, to graduation, v. 17).' The words 'given by inspiration of God' (v. 16) are (rightly) reduced in NIV, ESV to one word, 'God-breathed'. Divine inspiration is not a subsequent 'polish' or 'enhancement' given to an originally human production. The Scriptures began as truth God himself 'breathed out' and which was then brought to the Church through his chosen agents, and through them received its genuine human colorations without losing anything of its divine origin and quality.

LUKE'S INSIGHT

Luke 24:13–49, Luke's chosen revelation of the risen Lord Jesus, gives us an important insight into our Lord's view of the Old Testament. (1) The Risen Lord refuses to allow himself to be known (v. 16) except through the Holy Scriptures (vv. 27, 32). (2) The suggestion that the Scriptures were known in three parts ('Moses... the prophets...all the Scriptures', v. 27) is made explicit in verse 44, 'the Law of Moses...the Prophets and the Psalms.' The Hebrew Scriptures contain exactly those three sections and in that order, 'Psalms' being the first book in the third section ('the Writings'), here giving its name to the whole section. Compare Luke 11:51 where Jesus reviews the Old Testament 'martyrs' from Abel to Zechariah. Abel is recorded in the first book in the Hebrew Canon (Gen. 4) and Zechariah in 2 Chronicles 24:20–21, the last book in the Hebrew Canon. In a word, Jesus possessed and validated the Old Testament as we know it, the three-fold book comprising Genesis–2 Chronicles (though our OT follows the order of books in the Septuagint, the Greek translation of the Hebrew).

4

PREPARING FOR JESUS

Now this Old Testament, above all else we might say about it, is designed to prepare us for the Lord Jesus Christ. Or, putting the matter more bluntly, without the Old Testament, we could not know Jesus properly. That is important enough to repeat: without the Old Testament we could not know Jesus properly. Does that not make it supremely important for us? In days gone by we were taught to see the whole Bible focused on Jesus: the Old Testament is Jesus predicted; the Gospels are Jesus arrived; the Acts of the Apostles is Jesus preached; the Epistles are Jesus explained; the Revelation is Jesus coming again. And, as far as it goes, that does indeed encapsulate the great central reality of the Scriptures.

MATTHEW'S STARTING POINT

Remember how Matthew began his gospel? He began his gospel with a chapter full of 'begats' and 'begottens', and we find ourselves compelled to ask why. What is Matthew saying to us? He is saying that if we are to understand the birth of Jesus we do not start with the wonderful Mary, whom God chose to mother his Son, or with the courageous Joseph who allowed himself to be conscripted as an adopted father. No, 'the book of the genealogy (lit., birth) of Jesus Christ' (Matt. 1:1) must begin much earlier, with David and Abraham. This is how we are to understand his birth. We must go right back into the very depths of the Old Testament. This is his background, his pre-history.

Not only Matthew but the other three Gospels also make us face up to Jesus' pre-history. Mark takes us back through Malachi (Mark 1:2; Mal. 3:1; 4:5), to Isaiah (Mark 1:3; Isa. 40:3) and then to the forerunner himself, John the Baptist. Through Malachi's eyes, we see Jesus as the Lord himself come to his temple, heralded by the foretold 'Elijah'; for Isaiah he is the preacher of the word of consolation (Isa. 40:1), the divine Lord (40:3) with a message for 'all flesh' (40:5). He is also not on this occasion the political conqueror of the nations which the then current Judaism awaited, but the sort of Messiah for whom John's message of repentance, and the personal confession of sin were the proper preparation (Mark 1:4–5). Luke (3:38) strikes the note of universal significance by tracing our Lord's genealogy back to Adam, and, like Matthew, underlines the Davidic ancestry of Jesus (1:27, 32). John goes deepest of all: his gospel begins with the account of Jesus in heaven: Jesus, the Word, was not only 'with God' but 'was God'. More of all this later when we deal with prediction and fulfilment.

Matthew's Perspective: Abraham and David

Returning now to Matthew. His insistence is that we must see Jesus in the light of Abraham and David (Matt. 1:1). To Abraham was made the promise of blessing for the whole world (Gen. 12:1–3; 22:15–18). Also we must see him in the light of David to whom God promised that he would have a universal and eternal Kingdom (2 Sam. 7:16; Ps. 89:3–4, 20–29; Isa. 9:6–7). Those two things—a Kingdom that spread without limit and lasted without end—characterise the promised rule of David, and Matthew insists that we cannot truly understand Jesus unless we put on spectacles of which one lens focuses on Abraham and the other on David. In this way, before ever we come to Bethlehem we are made aware that the coming One will recover blessing for the whole world and is destined to rule every created reality for time and eternity. When we jump over that first chapter of Matthew we lose the excitement of it. But what it is telling us is this, that without the Old Testament, we cannot know Jesus properly.

And Isaiah

When Matthew, at the end of chapter one, turns to the birth of the Lord Jesus Christ, he adds another lens to our spectacles! Look at Jesus, not only through Abraham and David, but take another big character into account: the prophet Isaiah. In Matthew's view, we will not understand about Jesus until we read the words in Isaiah 7:14—'Behold the virgin shall conceive and bear a son and shall call his name Immanuel.' We see again how the whole Bible is coming together and how true it is that if we put our Old Testaments on one side, we are truncating our knowledge of Jesus. As well as being the One who will bless and rule the whole world, Jesus is also (Matt. 1:23) the foretold wonder Child of Virgin Birth, and, indeed, God himself come to be with us.

As against current opinion and liberal theology, the word 'virgin' in the Hebrew of Isaiah 7:14, as in the Greek of Matthew 1:23 does mean a virgin. It speaks to us about the miracle of the virgin birth. And Isaiah foresaw it, and it is part of his 'take' on the coming Messiah. It is part of his inspired testimony of Jesus. He is the virgin's Son. The miracle Child born of the miracle mother. He is also the miracle Child in another way because he is God with us. For further study on this great truth: Alec Motyer, *The Prophecy of Isaiah,* IVP. 1993, pp. 84–85; Isaiah, IVP. 1999, pp. 88, 90–91; Allan Harman, *Isaiah,* CFP. 2005, p. 87.

THE SEVENFOLD FULFILMENT

Beyond the birth of the Lord Jesus Christ, as Matthew develops the story leading up to the beginning of his public ministry, we find this same insistence on the Old Testament foundation as essential. We are bound to say that to read the New Testament at any point is an exercise that drives us back into the Old Testament. We cannot be genuine New Testament readers and believers without knowing, probing and understanding the Old. Look at Matthew's account, in 1:17–4:17, of the period between the birth of Jesus and the moment when he 'began to preach'. We can call these chapters 'The Book of the Seven Fulfilments', for Matthew picks up seven predictions of the Old Testament and uses them as a lens through which to get a full understanding of what Jesus is all about: the Child who was born of a virgin (1:22–23); his birth in Bethlehem (2:5–6); the flight to Egypt and the return (2:15); the slaughter of the innocents (2:17–18); settling in Nazareth (2:23); the ministry of John as Forerunner (3:1–3); and Jesus' own ministry starting in the far north, where the people who walked in darkness have seen a great light (4:13–14). You see, then, how Matthew (and indeed the whole of the New Testament, if we had time to do it) is insisting that without the Old Testament we do not know Jesus properly. The Old Testament lays down the ground rules, and the ground interpretation, and is the perfect lens through which to view the One who has come to be our Saviour. The Old Testament prepares us for the Lord Jesus. It is the Wonder Book of the Wonder Child born of the wonder mother, to be God with us.

5

BIBLE WORDS HAVE BIBLE MEANINGS

We move on now to another great truth about our Bibles: the Old Testament explains the New Testament. Without the Old Testament we would not understand our New Testament properly. The Old Testament lays down the basis on which we understand the main revelations that come to us from God in our New Testaments.

WORDS AND MEANINGS

Take the great words of our religion, for example, the really great words that surround the thought of redemption. What does redemption mean?

One approach would be to look the word up in a dictionary, and that might be helpful enough in its own way, but, as a matter of fact, 'redemption' is used in the New Testament on the assumption that we have read the Old Testament! To put this matter succinctly, Bible words have Bible meanings, and what matters to us is not the dictionary's opinion, but how a word is used in Scripture, what its basic meaning is, and what range of meanings is it used to cover.

REDEMPTION WORDS

So let's learn a bit of Hebrew. There are two, maybe three great words that surround redemption and it is the Old Testament that explains them to us. The first we will consider is the Hebrew word *Goel*. In the Book of Ruth, we read how Ruth with her mother-in-law, Naomi, came back to Bethlehem after a long period away from home in the land of Moab. Naomi had gone out full, she said, and the Lord had brought her back empty (1:21). This was true at one level, for she had left Bethlehem with a

One of the best friends to have in Bible reading and study is a good Concordance—a book (or computer software) that lists all the verses in which any given word occurs. *Cruden's Concordance* does no more than list words found in the AV. Young's 'Analytical Concordance' and Strong's 'Exhaustive Concordance' go further. Recognising that sometimes an English word may be used to translate or represent more than one Hebrew or Greek word, in effect they offer separate lists, linking the English word to the Hebrew and Greek of the original. In this way we can come to grips with the way the Bible actually uses its chosen vocabulary.

husband and two small boys, but she returned, bereaved
of her husband and both her sons, and one only of her
in-laws, Ruth, returned with her. There is, however, in
the book of Ruth, a deeper truth which can be put this
way, that she went out and the Lord brought her back.
This is part of the book's meaning: the sovereign care,
oversight, and detailed direction of our lives in the hands
of a loving, provident God.

THE RIGHT OF THE NEXT-OF-KIN

Naomi came back with her daughter-in-law Ruth, and
they were poverty stricken. In a day without social security,
the question was urgent: How were they to be provided
for? But the Lord had anticipated his people's needs, and
had made a provident regulation—the institution of the
'goel'. 'Here we are,' Naomi and Ruth could have said,
'with all these burdens. We need a *Goel*. We need (as
it is often explained) a "Kinsman-Redeemer". This, in
brief, was how the regulation worked. When a situation
of need arose in Israel, it was the right of the immediate
next-of-kin to come to the rescue, and say, 'Have you got
a debt? Let me pay it. Have you got a burden? Let me
bear it. Have you got a problem? Let me solve it. Have
you got a need? Let me meet it.' This was the institution
of the Kinsman-Redeemer.

As the story unfolds, Naomi and Ruth begin by taking
advantage of another, basic social provision: the custom
of allowing the poor to 'glean' the crops of the more
affluent (Lev. 19:10; 25:25; Deut. 24:19–22; Ruth 2:2). At

this point, see the loving providence of the Lord: Ruth, all-unknowing, went to glean in the field of Boaz—and Boaz was a close relative, 'a near kinsman' (Ruth 2:20)!

If you are getting a sense that 'the plot is thickening' you are right! Chapter 4 of Ruth records how seriously next-of-kinship was considered. As things turned out, Boaz would have willingly shouldered the responsibility of Naomi and Ruth, but, as he explained to the redeemer, 'There is no one to redeem it but you, and I am after you' (4:4). The redeemer expressed willingness to buy for himself the farmland that had belonged to Naomi's husband, but when he learned that Ruth was part of the package, he backed off—'I cannot redeem it for myself, lest I ruin my own inheritance' (4:6)—by which he presumably meant that the extra and on-going responsibility of Ruth and an additional family was more than his present means could undertake. So Boaz was the *goel*, the kinsman-redeemer, after all, and they all lived happily ever after!

It has been important to review the story of Ruth in this way because it makes the meaning of the word 'goel' unmistakeably clear. What, then, is this next of kin? What is this *Goel*? He's the one who has the right to say, 'You've got a problem. Give it to me. You've got a burden.

Other references to the *goel*. Job (19:25) knew that in his extremity of trouble he had a *goel* ('redeemer') who would guarantee his ultimate wellbeing. 'Redeemer' is one of the titles used of the Lord, and used by the Lord of himself (Ps. 19:14; 103:4; Isa. 41:14; 43:14; 44:24; 59:20; 60: 16; etc.).

Let me bear it. You've got a debt. Let me pay it as though it were mine. You've got a need. Let me meet it.' In this way, we are to understand the word redemption? This is precisely what the Lord meant when he allowed his Old Testament people to think of him as their Redeemer, and spoke of himself as such. This is exactly what Jesus has done: 'You've got a burden—your sin. Give it to me. You've got a debt in the sight of God. Let me pay it. You've got a need you cannot possibly meet. Let me meet it for you.' Do you see that clearly? Well, you would not have done so without the Old Testament and the Book of Ruth. Without the Old Testament we wouldn't understand, grasp this great truth of our New Testament in full reality.

That's the word *Goel*, then, but there is also another word, the Hebrew verb, *Padah*. *Padah* means 'to pay the price'. *Goel* stresses the person who does the paying, and *Padah* stresses the price that he has to pay. Whatever the price is, he will come along and pay it on behalf of the troubled, burdened, weary, helpless soul. Do I know these things because I happen to know a bit of Hebrew? No. We can all find them in a concordance—just look the word up and chase it through the Bible, and these meanings will come trotting out for you. It takes more

Some references for *padah*, 'to pay the ransom price'. Leviticus 27:27 (note the link between *padah* and 'valuation'), cf., Numbers 18:15–16; see the reference to cost in Psalm 49:7–8. Exodus 13:13. 'To redeem' is widely used of what the Lord has done for his people (e.g., Deut. 21:8; Ps. 25:22; 71:23; Isa. 35:10; etc.).

trouble than sitting and letting me tell you, of course, but you can do it! And you can prove what I am saying to you that without the Old Testament we cannot understand the New Testament properly.

ONE MORE WORD: KAPHAR

The verb *kaphar* may sound slightly familiar in that we hear of today's Jews celebrating 'yom kippur', the 'day of atonement'. What does *kaphar* mean? In its ordinary or secular use it means 'to cover over'. In Genesis 6:14 the Lord said to Noah to cover the Ark inside and outside with pitch. Hide the woodwork out of sight. Cover it over. And that's the vocabulary used in the Old Testament for atonement. The covering over of our sin so that it is out of sight, out of mind. But we must not think of this as a mere sweeping of sin under the carpet. If it were swept under the carpet, it would be out of sight but not out of mind. It would still be there. So think of it this way: a wife says to her husband, 'If you're going out this morning, will you go to the supermarket and get some goods?' And a wise and experienced husband will say, 'Yes, dear.' That's the ground work of a happy marriage! The husband always has the last word. He says, 'Whatever you think, dear.' 'Yes, dear. I will go to the supermarket provided that, (1) You give me a list, and (2) Have you got any money?' So he sallies off to the supermarket and loads his trolley with goods, but as he walks around, pushing his loaded trolley, none of the goods in it belongs to him—they all belong to whoever owns the supermarket, and they represent the amount he is in debt. At the checkout the assistant adds up the amount of the debt, the money is handed over, and the debt is 'covered'. Not in the sense of being swept under the carpet—'Let's say no more about it'—but in the sense of being killed off and finished, dead and done with, so that it can never raise its head again and make an accusation. It's gone! It's been paid. It's been covered!

Now is the Old Testament not, once more, illuminating the New for you? Here you have the *Goel* who comes alongside—the Lord Jesus. 'You've got a problem. Give it to me. It's mine.' *Padah*. 'There's a price to be paid. 'Alright. I'll pay it.' *Kaphar*. 'The price I pay will cover over your indebtedness so that it will never raise its head or be mentioned again.' Gone!

The Old Testament explains the New. Without the Old Testament, we cannot understand our New Testaments.

More references for *kaphar*: In its form as a 'simple active' verb, *kaphar* only occurs in Genesis 6:14. In its 'intensive active' form (*kipper*) it occurs about 90 times and almost always in the meaning 'to make atonement', but, of course, without losing its root meaning of 'cover over' sin in such a way that its debt is paid (Lev. 4:20, 26, 31, 35). Note Exodus 21:30 where the derived noun, *kopher* refers to a monetary 'ransom'; likewise Exodus 30:12 where it is translated 'ransom' and the money is specified in the following verse. The beautiful, emotive rendering 'mercy seat' (e.g., Exod. 25:17–22) really means 'covering' (*kapporeth*); in NIV 'atonement cover') because it received the sprinkled blood on the Day of Atonement (Lev. 16:14), the blood which paid the 'covering price'.

6

KNOWING GOD

We have looked at the way the Old Testament prepares for the Lord Jesus (ch. 3), and the way it provides basic explanations for the great New Testament truth of redemption (ch. 4). We consider now what is perhaps its deepest of all tasks: how the Old Testament reveals God in ways that the New Testament simply assumes and builds on. Without the Old Testament our knowledge of God would be incomplete.

GOD THE CREATOR

The New Testament makes no secret of the fact that the Lord God Almighty is God the Creator but in order to know what it means to call God the Creator, we must go back into the Old Testament. Indeed, our understanding of God the Creator is very limited if we fail to follow it through the Old Testament in order to discover its full truth. We automatically think of the Creator as the one who pushed the boat out in the beginning. Well, first of all, of course, he made the boat, and then He pushed it out, and that's the doctrine of Creation. No, no—that's only a quarter of it! Look up the verb 'to create' in a concordance and trace it through the Old Testament.

God the Creator is the God who begins everything, the God of origins. Throughout the Old Testament the verb 'to create' is exclusively God's verb. Wherever it is used with a grammatical subject, stated or implied, that subject is God. Unlike the situation in cognate languages, 'to create' is never used of artistic creativity; it only refers to God's activity in his creatorial work. Genesis 1 is a chapter full of origination. In verse 1 'create' is used to cover the total work of bringing heaven and earth into being, and in 2:3, retrospectively, of the same comprehensive task. It is used in 1:21 at the significant point when animate life was created, and it is used three times (vv. 26–27) of the creation of humankind in the image of God, marking out Man as the creature par excellence.

God the Creator maintains everything in existence—so that if for one split second he ceased to do so it would no longer be there, indeed even the spatial concept of 'there' would not exist! Isaiah 42:4 exemplifies Old Testament thinking with its use of four participles—in Hebrew, the participle represents an on-going, unchanging state of affairs, and (literally) the verse reads: 'This is what the (transcendent) God, Yahweh, has said—he who is creating the heavens and stretching them out, who is spreading out the earth and its produce, who is giving breath to the people on it.' There, in one verse, is the whole concept of the Creator as Maintainer. All the time, ceaselessly, moment by moment, he creates, stretches, spreads out, gives. The Lord Jesus took note of this when he said (John 5:17), 'My Father has been working until now, and I have been working.'

Thirdly, the Creator God controls everything in its operations. Nothing is out of His control. Possibly the most striking passage in this connection is Isaiah 54:16–17. According to verse 16a the Creator originated the technician or craftsman with some particular skill; in verse 16b the Creator is equally the source of the specific way in which the artefact in question is used; and in verse 17a the assurance is offered that the use of that artefact is wholly within the control of the Creator. Obviously, we are touching here on great mysteries, beyond our capacity to understand or explain. Read Isaiah 54:16–17 again but do so in the light (say) of modern weapons of warfare. It baffles us why the all-controlling God allows war, and the ferocious weapons human skill has devised, and the vile cruelty with which they are used. But remember that Isaiah knew all about war with no holds barred, accompanied by fiendish cruelty: he lived in the days of Assyrian imperialism! Yet he dared to write 54:16–17! No, we cannot explain it, but, yes, we can be glad it is so—even at its most appalling the world is still totally in the Creator's hand and control.

Fourthly, the Creator directs everything to the end he has determined for it. Listen out for the threefold use of 'create' in Isaiah 65:17–18. The verb is a participle each time: there is an on-going work of God which will result in the newness of God's new Creation: 'For behold, I create (am creating) new heavens and a new earth; and the former shall not be remembered or come to mind. But be glad and rejoice for ever in what I create (am creating). For behold, I create (am creating) Jerusalem as a rejoicing, and her people a joy.' The verb points to an exclusive work of God; its form as a participle proclaims its perpetual presence in the mind of God as his ceaseless object of interest and determination; its threeness, as in Genesis 1:27, indicates a creative work par excellence; and its newness is such as to dispel memory of what once was, and to anticipate it as a work of total delight and satisfaction to its inhabitants.

GOD'S WORLD

How very much fuller and more satisfying than simply thinking of the Creator in terms of making a beginning! The New Testament, of course, assumes this fourfold magnificence of God the Creator, but it is the Old Testament that spells it out for us. And it takes its own teaching seriously! This is why, for example, the Psalms so often take time to remind us that the Lord is the Maker of heaven and earth. Psalm 104 is a rhapsody on Genesis 1; Psalm 33:6–9 affirms the heavens and the earth as the product of the creative Word of God (cf., 148:5) and, typically of Psalms of Creation, ends (v. 21) by an allusion to the Creator's holiness (cf., 104:35). In Psalm 121:1 the writer might be a pilgrim thinking of the perilous, robber-infested hill-terrain through which he must pass on his way to the city of God; he might be a resident of Jerusalem looking apprehensively at the surrounding hills over which, presently, some enemy will approach—we are not told what his problem was, so that we may fill in the blank with whatever our fear or anxiety may be on any given occasion. But, in the light of the threatening future, see what he does: he turns to 'the Lord who made heaven and earth', the God who initiates, maintains, controls and directs everything in his whole creation. What a comfort! Every threat that comes to us comes in his world, arises and exists by his will, is controlled within his sovereignty, and is designed to achieve his purpose. We are safe!

His Story

On the larger scale, the Creator controls and directs the whole course of world history. He is the God of history. It is 'his story'. Nothing happens outside of his hand and say-so. Never be afraid to exalt the sovereignty of God to the nth degree and beyond. It's the pillow on which we can lay our heads. We are only safe in this world because it's His world, and the Bible assures us of his creatorial governance of what he has made. A key passage on this topic is Isaiah 10:5–15. Assyria was the then world super-power, bent on sweeping as much of the world as possible into its empire. Do not be concerned that all the Assyrians had were bows and arrows, chariots and horses; that was all anyone had at the time—and Assyria had more than the others, coupled with more determination, ferocity and unscrupulousness. As he contemplated the Assyrian threat, Isaiah saw two 'forces' in balance: on the one hand, there was Yahweh's moral motive to punish ungodly Judah (v. 6); on the other hand, by contrast, there was Assyria's imperialistic determination to conquer (vv. 7–11)—a sinful determination which would be punished in its own time (vv. 11–14). Assyria's decision in the matter was a real decision, a real personal responsibility, else why would the holy God foretell punishment? But Yahweh's power was sovereign; indeed, so much so that Isaiah does not hesitate to depict Yahweh as the woodman and Assyria as the axe, Yahweh as the carpenter, Assyria as the saw—a mere tool in the hands of the sovereign God. Because Yahweh is God, his is the 'whip hand'. It must be so. But the Assyrian's motives, choices and decisions too are real.

All history is like that, the Old Testament would teach us. Divine sovereignty is real: God is the Creator God, initiating, maintaining, controlling, directing; human responsible choice is real, deciding, planning, executing, being morally responsible and answerable. Can we reconcile these two 'forces'? No, it is not given to us to plot their inner relationships and out-workings, and all Isaiah does is hint at an illustration (37:29), that of a horse and its rider. In English show-jumping it seems a matter of indifference whether a commentator says that the horse has had a clear round or the rider has had a clear round, yet each, without the other, would not get round at all, clear or otherwise! Two 'forces' are present: the horse for power, the rider for direction, and that is all we can say. In history, human choices are real, and decision-makers are answerable; Yahweh's determination and direction reign supreme.

God's Moral Government of the World

This chapter has already become too long, but one more thing must be said. The Old Testament gives us good grounds for affirming the moral order that undergirds all history. We cannot always trace out the ways of God, but his ways are always right, fair, and just.

Before the Lord visited the world with flood, or Sodom with fire, he carried out a moral audit of the situation to see what was merited (Gen. 6:5–7; 18:20–21).

We are rightly horrified by the divine command to exterminate the existing Canaanite population (Deut. 7:1–5; 20:16–18; Josh. 6:17,21; etc.) but even this is represented as a just and justified action of moral retribution. We read in Genesis 15:16 that the gift of the land to Abram's

We would wish that the 'slaughter of the Canaanites' were not in the Bible, but that is not the right question. The question is do we want a world ruled by the Lord's moral ordinances or a world in which iniquity is never brought to book. It is the Old Testament which assures us that the world we live in is the latter, and which summons us to trust the Lord in all his ways.

descendants would be delayed for four generations because 'the iniquity of the Amorites is not yet complete'. Simply to dispossess people of their land is not right, but the all-seeing eye of holiness discerns a time four hundred years hence when moral deserving will merit disinheritance and death, and at that moment Joshua and his forces will be knocking at the door.

7

FOLLOWING THE STRAIGHT LINE

Taking up an attitude of prayer, read Psalm 119:17–24.
The Bible says:

> Deal bountifully with your servant that I may live and keep
> your Word. Open my eyes that I might see wondrous things
> in your law. I am a stranger on earth. Do not hide your
> commandments from me. My soul breaks with longing for
> your judgements at all times. You rebuke the proud, accursed
> who stray from your commandments. Remove from me
> reproach and contempt for I have kept your testimonies.
> Princes also sit and speak against me but your servant
> meditates on your statutes. Your testimonies also are my
> delight and my counsellors.

Can you think of the Old Testament as a straight line? It starts with the Creation in Genesis, then we meet with Abraham, then the Exodus and Moses, the people of God coming to the promised land, the period of the Judges. Samuel, the final judge, comes on the scene; then they decide that they need and want a king. After the failure of the first king, Saul, the chosen king after God's own heart (1 Sam. 13:14; Acts 13:22) is David. You see how we can trace a straight line? Extend that line on through the prophets, through the kings—in the southern kingdom of Judah, the kings in the line of David; in the northern kingdom of Israel, the series of episodic monarchies of rival aspirants to the throne. Now try to go on, beyond our Old Testament: where does our line come out?

The Old Testament is, in many ways, a book standing on tiptoe, straining forward into the future. God gave Abraham a promise (Gen. 12:1–3; 22:15–17; cf., 26:4) that he would be heir of the world, and bring back the blessing that the world had lost: he was looking forward to see the fulfilment of the promise, but fulfilment did not come in the Old Testament. Moses spoke of 'a Prophet like unto me' (Deut. 18:14–18), but Deuteronomy 34:10 records that no such prophet has arisen. David was promised a kingship over all Creation, for all time (Ps. 89:19–29), but the Old Testament ends still waiting for the coming of that King. So where is it all going? Where is the other end of the line?

The line from the Old Testament runs straight into the New Testament. Have you got that? Not anywhere else—straight into the New Testament.

MALACHI AND MATTHEW

Malachi, the last of the prophets, worked in or around 400 years before Jesus. And, in our Bibles, next to come on the scene is Matthew. Malachi (3:1; 4:5) envisaged the fore-runner to prepare for the Lord's messianic advent; Matthew tells us that that fore-runner was John the Baptist. So Malachi and Matthew form a direct link, the straight line without any deviation, straight from the Old Testament to the New.

In the 400 years between Malachi and Matthew an offshoot developed and became what in the time of the Lord Jesus was Pharisaic Judaism. The Lord Jesus, warned that he has displeased the Pharisees, responded about them that they were a plant which his heavenly Father did not plant (Matt. 15:12–13). Now, if we were to put that into other words in context, we would describe Pharisaic Judaism as an Old Testament heresy, an offshoot that came to development between Malachi and Matthew, between what we call the Old and New Testaments, and then continued on its way in a parallel line to the straight line of Holy Scripture.

So what?

The implication of the 'straight line'—Malachi straight through into Matthew—is that the Old Testament as we call it belongs to us. It is our book. It runs straight into the New Testament, to the Lord Jesus and all those who belong to him. Our Bibles, then, are one book bound together from beginning to end. The Old Testament does not belong—let me say it to you sensitively—does not belong to the Jewish people. The Old Testament is our book, and the things that happened in the Old Testament are our prehistory, yours and mine because we belong to Jesus. Bishop Maurice Wood was the prince of pulpit anecdotes. 'A story for every occasion' could be the title of his biography. He delighted to tell of a Frenchman who became a naturalised Englishman. He was asked, 'Has it made any difference to you that you are now an English citizen and not a French citizen?' 'Oh yes,' he said, 'it has made all the difference in the world. You see now I've won the Battle of Waterloo!' The Old Testament is our book. We should never find ourselves saying 'They came out of Egypt.' The Exodus redemption is my prehistory and yours. And what we call Old and New Testament is one magnificent story of God working out his age-long purpose of salvation, making promises and keeping them, inspiring predictions and fulfilling them, taking and preserving a people for his name and glory.

SOME SIGNIFICANT VERSES

In the light of this review of the Old Testament, and the visual image of the 'straight line', consider these verses.

Galatians 3:29: 'If you are Christ's, then you are Abraham's seed, and heirs according to the promise.' We who trust the Lord Jesus Christ can call Abraham our father. The word 'seed' is important because it is a key word in the Abrahamic promises. The 'seed' are the chosen ones who inherit all that was pledged to their father. Romans 9:6–7 argues that mere physical descent from Abraham has never been the vital factor. Isaac was the child of promise, and all who are in Christ share in that privileged status (Gal. 4:28, 31–5:1). A distinction that prevails all through the Old Testament is made explicit in Isaiah 8:11–18. There is a true community of the Lord's own within the professing people. They are distinctive (v. 11), devoutly aware of the holiness of their God (v. 13), and know him as their security ('sanctuary', v. 14). They preserve the 'testimony …the law' (v. 16); they wait and hope in the Lord, and 'speak according to this word' (v. 20). In a word, they are the genuinely believing community, holding on to and preserving the Word of God, the true forebears of those who now believe in Jesus.

Galatians 6:16 describes us as 'the Israel of God', that is to say, Israel as God always intended Israel to be. The people of Antioch, who, historians say, had the habit of contriving 'nicknames', were the first to call the people of Jesus 'Christians' (Acts 11:26). It is a fair title, but we should never have allowed it the exclusive currency it enjoys. We should have insisted on our proper and true title, 'Israel'— the 'Israel of God' because we belong to Jesus.

Philippians 3:3: 'We are the circumcision'—not the true circumcision, as contrasted with the false; not the real as compared with the unreal; but the only ones who bear the mark of those to whom God has pledged his covenant promises. In the Old Testament circumcision was the visible mark of grace. Now it belongs to us. We are the marked out people.

Colossians 2:11–12: 'You were also circumcised with the circumcision…of Christ, buried with him in baptism.' Just as circumcision was the mark of grace in the Old Covenant, baptism is the mark of grace in the New Testament, the mark of God on those who are his. As Covenant signs, circumcision and baptism speak of the promises of God and symbolize the donation of those promises to authorised candidates, but, as promises, they only modulate into the spiritual realities of which they speak by the sovereign decision of God and the exercise of personal faith. We are within the embrace of the covenant, marked with its 'sign', which, as a 'sign', both speaks volumes of the saving grace of God in Christ, and, encapsulating the word of God, partakes of the distinctiveness of that word not to return void.

THE PEOPLE OF THE BOOK

How wonderfully important this is! The Old Testament is not something that we try to accommodate ourselves to as though it were an alien book, belonging to somebody else and only ours at second hand. It is our book. In the persons of our ancestors we were at the Passover. The lamb was slain for us. We sheltered under the blood. We came out from Egypt. We are the inheritors of the promises of God. The Old Testament is not an alien country. It is not somebody else's property. It is our property. We, because we belong to Jesus, are the Israel of God.

8

THE GREAT UNITIES:
ONE BOOK, ONE COVENANT

THE INDIVISIBLE BIBLE

I know that this will sound like a childish game, but I promise you it is seriously meant. You will probably not want actually to do it to your Bible; just do it in your mind. Bibles are always published with a title page between the end of Malachi and the beginning of Matthew. It announces (in my NIV) 'The New Testament', but often, in older printings, the fuller statement 'The New Testament of our Lord and Saviour Jesus Christ.' My 'game' is this: suppose you took that page out, where would you put it back? Well, for a start, not between Malachi and Matthew! Just think: Malachi foretells the coming of the forerunner (3:1; 4:5). Matthew announces that the forerunner has arrived (3:1). Plainly, it is mistaken to insert a page holding those two books apart! So where will we put our dividing page? Actually, wherever we try to insert the divider, even the single fact of prediction and fulfilment will say that we have got it wrong. I find the dividing page a waste of paper and print. It is separating the inseparable, dividing the indivisible. The Bible is one book.

THE COVENANT AND THE COVENANTS

There are great unities which bind the Bible into one. Prediction and fulfilment is one of them, and it will concern us later on. We make a start here with the central Bible theme of God's Covenant with his people.

Noah

The word 'covenant' appears for the first time in the Bible in Genesis 6:18, and is addressed to Noah. Literally, 'I will cause my covenant to stand up', meaning 'I will activate/implement my covenant'. The covenant is thus an existing understanding between God and Noah: in context this must mean that in the light of the impending divine judgment of flood, God intends to activate his promise to keep Noah safe. God's covenant is his promise of salvation from his just judgment. God's judgment is his considered response to his examination of the evidence, Genesis 6:5–7, where all (note the repeated word, 'man') have sinned and all must die. But, in Noah's case, a new factor comes into operation: (v. 8) 'Noah found grace'. Wherever this expression is used (e.g., 47:25; Ruth 2:10) the implication is of the inferior, supplicatory, even meritless status of the one 'finding grace', and, certainly in Noah's case, in the context of verses 5–7, the perfectly accurate translation 'Noah found grace' must mean 'grace found Noah'. Like the rest of mankind, Noah is involved in wickedness (v. 5), is the object of divine sorrow (v. 6), and is subject to God's decree of judgment (v. 7), but 'grace' intervened. God's covenant, therefore, is an outreaching of grace, with a promise of salvation, to those by nature under judgment.

Abraham

In Romans 4:15 Paul lays down the principle that 'where there is no law there is no transgression.' This was the case all through the era of the patriarchs in Genesis, and, indeed, right through to the giving of the law through Moses (Exod. 20). Consequently in God's covenant dealing with Abraham, sin is not a primary concern. First, the Lord presents himself to Abram as the great promise maker (Gen. 15). The (to us) curious incident of creating a pathway between the divided animals (vv. 9–10) is explained in Jeremiah 34:18 as a ceremony of covenanting: did they understand it as a visible way of saying, 'If I break my covenant, so may it be done to me and my beasts'? At any rate, in Genesis 15:17, the Lord uses the symbols of smoke and fire (cf., Exod. 13:21; 19:18) to indicate his presence, and he alone passes between the severed pieces; he alone is the oath-taker, he alone makes the covenant promise, and intends to see it through, even implying that he will bear the penalty should the covenant be broken. What, then, is the covenant promise thus sealed by sacrifice (15:18)? It is spelled out in Genesis 17:1-8—a personal and domestic promise of transformation (vv. 4-5), a royal promise of coming kings (v. 6), a spiritual promise to be God to Abraham and his descendants (lit., 'seed'), and a territorial promise of possession (v. 8).

Moses

The Lord sketched out to Abraham that covenant membership carried life-style implications with it (Gen. 17:1), but the requirement was left undeveloped, because, in the Lord's intended scheme, the giving of the detailed law was reserved for Moses at Sinai (Exod. 19-24). We can think of the whole historical movement from Egypt to Sinai to Canaan as a gigantic visual aid. According to Exodus 6:7 the Lord's purpose and promise was to 'take you as my people, and I will be your God.' More, then, was involved than simply liberation from Egypt. The covenant relationship was to be established (Gen. 17:7-8; Deut. 4:20). Not only therefore would he free them from Egypt; he would 'redeem' them. This was what happened at Passover (Exod. 12). The Lord had sent nine plagues on the Egyptians to manoeuvre them into obedience. When they failed their probation, a new situation had to be faced; the dread tenth plague was different. Previously, the Lord has 'sent' plagues, but, this time, 'I will go out into the midst of Egypt' (Exod. 10:4) … 'I will pass through the land of Egypt…I will execute judgment' 12:12). When the Lord himself comes to judge, it is no longer Israel's relation to Pharaoh that matters, but how will they fare in the day of divine judgment. 'Grace' is not specifically mentioned, but surely it was divine grace which provided the sheltering blood which kept Israel safe on Passover night (Exod. 12: 7, 13, 22–3). Before Passover they could not leave Egypt; after Passover they could not stay, and, as the Lord's redeemed, pilgrim people, they set out for the promised land. Led by the great Pillar of Cloud and Fire so that they could not miss their way (Exod. 13:21–2), they were conducted, not to Canaan, but to Sinai. Are you interpreting the 'visual aid'? Egypt first, then Sinai; Passover first, then the giving of the Law; the divine work of grace first, then the life of responsive obedience, redemption/salvation first, then walking with God in his appointed way of holiness.

In the Old Testament, in God's revelation though Moses, as in the New Testament, in the divine Covenant, the Law is not a ladder of merit we attempt to climb in order to win God's favour; it is God's pattern of holy living given to us because, by redemption, we are already in his favour. It is not a way of salvation by works of obedience; it is a pattern of obedience divinely provided for those who have been saved by grace.

David

When the people asked for a king, it was, undoubtedly a departure from the pure way of faith in Yahweh (1 Sam. 8:7). Hitherto, when some national crisis arose, the Lord had raised up a 'judge' to deliver them (e.g., Judges 3:15), but, in the course of time, this seems to have proved too much of a strain, and a permanent monarchy seemed the logical solution. Again we are bound to introduce the idea of amazing divine grace: not only did the Lord accede to their felt need, and not only did he overlook the hurt to himself, he made monarchy the mode of his coming messianic blessings! David (as we have seen) was promised a kingdom unending in space and time (poetically expressed in Psalm 89:19–29), and the messianic theme was elaborated by the prophets into the expectation of a coming 'David' (Ezek. 34:24), or a 'branch' in David's family 'tree' (Jer. 23:5–6), a coming divine Messiah (Isa. 9:6), the 'Arm of the Lord' (53:1)— this is to say, the Lord himself with his sleeves rolled up for action (52:10). Psalm 89:3 allows us to think of a 'covenant' with David, and Isaiah (55:3) speaks of this covenant, extended to all who respond to the great gospel invitation (55:1), as an 'everlasting covenant' bringing to us the benefits of 'my faithful love promised to David'.

Jeremiah

Isaiah (54:10) and Ezekiel (37:26–7) both forecast the messianic future in terms of a 'covenant of peace'. In

Isaiah this arises from the Servant's peace-making death (53:5); Ezekiel sees the peace of the future centred on the Lord's 'dwelling' among his people (cf., Exod. 29:44–6). Jeremiah, however, was the one actually to use the expression 'new covenant' (31:31–4). As he foresaw it, in what does this newness consist? The 'law'—the Lord's teaching and direction for living—remains the same, but (a) it is now written not on stone tablets but on the heart. This is a dramatic way of saying that God's intended new covenant includes a work of regeneration: giving us a new nature to match the requirements of God's law/teaching; a heart designed for obedience. And (b), something Jeremiah does not explain (though Isaiah 53 does)— our sins and iniquities are so completely dealt with that they are even blotted out of the divine memory. In other words, in its final form, God's covenant rests on a full, complete, finished work of salvation, which, of course, is what Jesus said in summary when he spoke of 'the new covenant in my blood' (Lk. 22:20; cf., Heb. 10:12–18).

9

THE GREAT UNITIES: ONE GOD

We have already used Old Testament teaching about God the Creator to illustrate the way the two Testaments belong together, and how the New Testament takes on board what the Old Testament reveals.

CUMULATIVE REVELATION

The Bible as a whole is often described as 'progressive revelation', that is to say, the whole truth is not necessarily revealed on the first, or earlier, occasions it is mentioned but is progressively unfolded in the course of time. This is part of what Hebrews 1:1 means when it says that God spoke through the prophets in various portions and in different ways. No one prophet had all the truth; truth was 'progressively' revealed. My personal preference is to speak of 'cumulative' revelation. It would be possible to see the word 'progressive' as registering an advance from a 'primitive' to a 'mature' understanding, leaving the 'primitive' behind. This is not what happens in the Bible: hence the word 'cumulative' is preferable. Truth is built up layer upon layer, so that nothing is lost. The earlier statement is not primitive but partial—part of the complete whole that is yet to be.

'The Lord our God. The Lord is one!' (Deut. 6:4)

This, at any rate, is what happens over the course of the whole Bible, from the 'one God' in the Old Testament to God the Holy Trinity in the New. When Moses instructed our ancestor Israelites to make the confession 'The Lord is one' he had to decide which of two Hebrew words to use for 'one'. There is the word *yahid* which occurs in Genesis 22:2, where God refers to 'your son, the one and only/the unique/singular...Isaac' (cf., Judges 11:34; Jer. 6:26). Abraham had at least one other son, but Isaac was the unique child of promise, through whom alone the covenant line would continue. He was a sole 'one'. Moses did not choose that word, however, when he spoke about God, but rather the other word, *'ehad*, with a wholly different range of possibility. While *'ehad* mostly means a singular one (e.g., Gen. 19:9; 44:28; Ps. 106:11), it is also used where 'one' comprises other entities within its unity. Thus, in Genesis 2:24, 'they shall become one flesh'; cf., 'one people' (comprising two previously separate national identities, Genesis 34:16); a particularly fine example occurs in Exodus 26:6 where all its multiplicity of components which made up the Tabernacle came together 'so that it may be one tabernacle' (cf.,v. 11; 36:13, 18; Ezek. 37:17).

THE LORD OF HOSTS

It is against this background that we should understand the great title accorded to the Lord, familiar in the older English Versions, lost in NIV, retained in ESV, 'the Lord of hosts'. The question has to be asked what sort of genitive relationship 'of hosts' expresses. Does it simply express 'possession' and, if so, in what sense does 'the Lord' (better 'Yahweh') possess these hosts—and what are they? There are, however, a number of occasions where the fuller expression 'Yahweh, God of hosts' occurs. Usually 'God' is in a 'construct' or genitive relation, requiring the translation 'God of hosts', but there are some examples where 'God' and 'hosts' are what is called nouns in apposition which would require the translation 'Yahweh, God who is hosts'. That is to say, Yahweh's divine 'oneness' itself comprises 'hosts'. It is a 'multiple oneness' held together in a true unity. Notwithstanding that these instances are few in comparison with the hundreds of times 'Yahweh of hosts' occurs, they could well be the clue we need for interpreting the 'genitive' 'of hosts', namely that it is a genitive of explanation. Without a doubt, this offers by far the best understanding of the prophets' almost addiction to the name and title, 'Yahweh of hosts'. They had no interest in thinking of 'hosts' as referring to the armies of Israel (for which they had no concern, indeed the reverse), but a true enhancement of the divine nature would have been meat and drink to them.

References to 'Yahweh, the God who is hosts' (though the point is only evident in Hebrew, not in English versions), are Psalm 59:5 (6); 80:4,7,14,19 (5, 8, 15, 20).

THE ANGEL OF THE LORD

Throughout the Old Testament we met with angels (e.g, Gen. 19:1,15; 32:1; Ps. 103:20; Zech. 1:9,13), but, alongside this general revelation of the existence of angelic beings, there is a very special personage called 'The Angel of the Lord'.

The Angel is both an independent person (e.g., Gen. 16:7–12) and also is recognised as Yahweh revealing himself (e.g., Gen. 16:13). He speaks as in his own right (Gen. 22:15–18), repeating Yahweh's promises. He is both 'the Angel' (Exod. 3:2) and Yahweh ('the LORD') (Exod. 3:4), the God of the fathers (Exod. 3:6). Many of the other references confirm this understanding of the Angel, so that writers on the Old Testament speak of him as 'the double of Yahweh' or 'Yahweh's alter ego', 'a distinction without a difference'.

The Angel came to reveal Yahweh's reactions/purposes/ commands (Gen. 16:7–16), to reaffirm Yahweh's promises (Gen. 22:15–16), to intercede (Zech. 1:11–12).

Though 'the Angel' is 'the LORD' (Yahweh)—striking people with awe such as only the divine holiness can effect (Judges 13:6, 21–22), bearing the divine Name (Exod. 23:20–21), whose coming is the coming of the Lord himself (Mal. 3:1), yet he also represents some 'accommodation' to the human situation (Exod. 33:2–3). It is an outreaching of mercy (without any 'diluting' of his full divine nature). Even when he appears, sword in hand, his essential purpose is mercy (Num. 22:31–33).

When anyone saw the Angel of the Lord, they saw him as a man (e.g., Judges 13:6ff), none of the angelic 'trappings' of church tradition—such as a winged form. We can relate this to Genesis 1:27 and the creation of 'man' in the image of God. Put it this way: in his essential nature God is Spirit, and invisible, but when he wishes to clothe his invisibility in an outward shape, there is a form uniquely suited to his nature. It was in that form he created 'man'. Hence, even the human form of the Angel itself marks him out as God become visible.

This revelation of 'the Angel of the Lord' thus leads us back to Creation, but it also leads us forward to Jesus. Where else in Scripture is there one who is both distinct from Yahweh and identical with him; who, without losing or even diminishing his divine essence and holiness, yet

References to 'The Angel of the Lord': Gen. 16:7–14; 21:17–19; 22:11–18; 31:11–13; 32:24–30 (cf., Hos. 12:4); 48:15–16; Exod. 3:2–6; 14:19–22 (cf., 13:21; 14: 24); 23:20–22; 32:34 (cf., 33:2); Num. 22:22–35; Judges 2:1–5; 5:28; 6:11–22; 13: 2–23; 2 Sam. 24:16–17; 1 Kgs. 19:7; 2 Kgs. 1:13–15; 19:35; 1 Chr. 21:12–30; Isa. 37:36; 63:8–9; Dan. 3:28; 6:22; Zech. 1:11; 3:1–6; 12:8.

accommodates himself to the company of sinners; who can both affirm the wrath of God and at the same time be the supreme outreaching of divine mercy? Who but Jesus? The Angel is a chief Old Testament pre-view of the Second Person of the Trinity.

THE SPIRIT OF GOD

The verb most frequently used of the Spirit of God in the Old Testament is the verb 'to be'. It is usually represented in English as 'came upon' (Num. 24:2; Judges 3:10; 11:29; 1 Sam. 19:20, 23; 2 Chr. 15:1; 20:14), but it is better understood as 'became a living reality to'—the active reality of the Spirit evident in inspired words, mighty deeds, ecstatic 'prophesyings', or a sudden word from God.

The second most frequent verb is *tsalach*, whose meaning is not wholly clear. 'To penetrate', 'to rush upon', 'to be strong' all have their advocates. In Judges 14:6, 19; 15:14, the NKJV offers 'came mightily upon', but in 1 Samuel 10:6; 11:6; 16:13 simply 'came upon'. The uniting thought in all these reference is the presence of the Spirit as an irresistible force, whether in mighty deeds or in an overwhelming ecstatic experience.

Used only three times, there is the verb 'to wear/put on', used in the sense of Judges 6:34, 'the Spirit took (or put on) Gideon as a garment' (cf., 1 Chr. 12:18; 2 Chr. 24:20).

Other verbs for the most part are used only once of the activities of the Spirit of God: Numbers 11:25–6 ('rested'), 29 ('put', lit., 'gave'), Judges 13:25 ('began to move', lit., 'impelled'), 2 Samuel 23:2 ('spoke'), Nehemiah 9:20

('instruct'), Proverbs 1:23 ('pour out'), Isaiah 32:15 (a different verb, 'pour out'), 44:3 (another verb 'pour out'), Ezekiel 11:5 ('fell upon'), 39:29 (another 'pour out', also Joel 2:28,29).

Other Old Testament revelations of the nature and work of the Spirit of God include:

1. The Spirit in Creation (Gen. 1:2; Ps. 33:6; 104:30). The life-giver for all peoples (Isa. 42:5; cf., Job 27:3, NJKV 'breath'), and the life-terminator (Isa. 40:70).
2. The Spirit and the omnipresence of God (Ps. 139:7). Note how in the second line of this verse, 'Spirit' is paralleled by 'presence' (lit., 'face'). A person's face is a very personal indicator of presence: the Spirit is the very personal presence of God in every place.

We may add here other related issues in the revelation of the Spirit. In Ezekiel's opening vision, the four 'living creatures' represent the whole of created life (1:10): the 'man', the crown of creation; the lion, the greatest of wild beasts, the ox, the greatest of domesticated beasts, and the eagle as the greatest of flying creatures. Their constant motion (vv. 12–14) depicts the ceaseless ebb and flow of life on earth. Over all this complex flux of history the enthroned God sits as sovereign (vv. 26–27); his sovereign control is expressed in his word (vv. 25); but the Agent of his sovereign rule is his Spirit (vv. 20–21). With this we can compare Genesis 1:1–3 where we meet in turn God, his word and his Spirit. In Genesis 6:34, notwithstanding ambiguities in the way the verse is to be translated, God, by his Spirit, is in antagonism to the moral situation in the world—an anticipation of the 'good Spirit' of Nehemiah 9:20, the 'holy Spirit (Ps. 51:11), and the grieved Spirit (Isa. 63:10).

Throughout the Old Testament individuals were endowed with the Holy Spirit for specific times and tasks: Bezalel (Exod. 31:3), Othniel (Judges 3:10), Gideon (Judges 6:34), Jephthah (Judges 11:29), Samson (Judges 13:25), Saul (1 Sam. 11:6). This corresponds to the episodic 'filling' with the Holy Spirit in Acts (e.g., 1:4; 4:8; 4:31). David enjoyed an on-going experience of the Spirit (1 Sam. 16:13), and this is the implication of the 'resting' of the Spirit in Numbers 11:16–17, 24–6, 29). The Old Testament looks forward to outpourings of the Spirit on a hitherto unrealised scale in the foreseen (messianic) age: Isaiah 32:15; 44:3; 59:21; Ezekiel 39:29; Joel 2:28–9.

I should apologise for this rather scrappy presentation of the Old Testament revelation of the Spirit of God, and for such huge amount of references, but there seemed no other way of getting such a quantity of material into a reasonably short space, and I do appeal that you look up the references. They obviously bring you face to face with the divine Spirit, the Spirit who is the presence of God worldwide, and the Spirit who, while being divine and one with the Lord, is also a distinct entity with distinct functions, and a Person, not an impersonal force.

WORD AND WISDOM

The word of God is the effective, creative word which God speaks (Gen. 1:3,9, etc.), and also a quasi-independent 'messenger' which God sends (Ps.147:15; Isa.55:10–11). In Proverbs 8 Wisdom is certainly depicted in very personal terms, and we are possibly intended to understand a distinct divine Person alongside the Creator God. Whether this is so or not, certainly Word and Wisdom, along with the Angel of the Lord and the Spirit of God are meant to spell out something about the 'hosts' that infill (so to speak) the oneness of the one Lord.

THE HOLY TRINITY INCOGNITO

Many people seem to assume that the God revealed in the Old Testament is 'God the Father', awaiting the unveiling of God the Son and God the Holy Spirit in the New Testament, and so completing the revelation of God as Holy Trinity. This is a profoundly mistaken view of the Bible. Even the bare fact that John 12:38 sees Jesus as the fulfilment of Isaiah 53:1 should warn us against making the Old Testament the province of only God the Father! No, no, the God of the Old Testament is 'the Lord of hosts', the God whose unity is a rich diversity, as yet unfocused and undefined. But as soon as we enter the New Testament, as by a simple adjustment of the focusing lens, we are allowed to be present when the voice of the Father addresses his Son, when Jesus is identified as the Son of God, and when the Holy Spirit descends, bodily as a dove, to rest on Jesus and remain with him. And in that incomparably beautiful and simple way, the 'hosts' are brought into their correct and final focus, the 'incognito' is over, and the Holy Trinity is at last revealed.

10

THE GREAT UNITIES:

ONE WAY OF SALVATION

Psalm 51:1–3 are as good a starting point for this new chapter as we are likely to find. The psalm-title locks it firmly into the heart of the Old Testament, but its content is so plainly at home in the New Testament that it perfectly illustrates our theme.

NINE GREAT WORDS

In verses 1–3 there are nine leading words which fall into three groups of three:

1. Three words for what sin is: sin, iniquity, transgression. 'Sin' is the word for the specific offence (thought, word, deed, whatever). It is what we have in mind when we say 'I'm sorry for that'; 'iniquity' derives from a verb meaning 'to be bent', and points to the inner defect or warp in human nature which is the well-spring of all sin; 'transgression' translates the serious word 'rebellion', as of a subordinate against an overlord (e.g., 2 Kgs. 3:7).

2. Three words describing what God is: mercy, loving kindness, tender mercy: 'mercy' is (lit.,) 'grace', the unmerited, undeserved kindness of God—in the case of Noah (Gen. 6:8) the Lord's sheltering mercy in the day of judgment; 'loving kindness' and 'tender mercy' are respectively, 'steadfast love' and 'compassion', the love which is expressed by a decision of will (the 'I will' of the wedding service; committed love), and the love which makes the heart beat faster (romantic, passionate love; the love of 'falling in love').

3. Three words describing what is sought from God: blot out, wash thoroughly, cleanse: 'blot out' implies sin as a 'black mark' which God can see and which he can wipe away; 'wash thoroughly' is a 'launderer's' verb, ingrained dirt requiring a detergent which can reach right down into the fibres (cf., Heb. 9:14); 'cleanse' is mostly used in Leviticus (e.g., 13:6) and deals with sin as a defilement which separates the sinner from the holy God.

PASSOVER

It is plain that this understanding of sin, God and Salvation concurs with what we find in the New Testament, and in particular with what we experience in Jesus. Psalm 51:7 leads us in the other direction: 'purge (more lit., 'de-sin') me with hyssop' connects back with Exodus 12:7, 22. 'Hyssop' is the sprinkling instrument, applying the blood under which Israel sheltered in the night of divine judgment; in David's case, in the psalm, his sins (adultery and accessory to murder, 2 Sam. 12) had no corresponding provision in the code of sacrifices, but the reference to 'hyssop' means that somehow he discerned that God knew of a blood which could, in such cases, be applied to and avail for the sinner.

On Passover night the efficacy of the blood of the lamb was the key factor in salvation (Exod. 12:12–13, 22–3). A new situation had developed: during the period of Egypt's probation, God had sent nine plagues, but now the period of probation is over; their persistence in disobedience had carried them outside the days of divine patience; in the case of the tenth plague, which would prove effective (Exod. 11:1), the Lord himself would enter Egypt to exact judgment (Exod. 11:44–7; 12:12). How is this novel turn of events to be faced? No more is it a case of how the people will face up to Pharaoh. The question now is, whether there is a place of security when the Lord himself comes in judgment. How to stand before a holy God!

The Sheltering Blood

What did the blood of the lamb achieve, and why was it so extraordinarily efficacious in the hour of judgment? We can spell out the answer in four key ideas:

Safety (or Security). The Lord came to Egypt in judgment, but, taking refuge in their blood-marked houses, Israelites were safe. It was the blood that made all the difference (Exod. 12: 13, 22–23). What saved them was not divine favouritism, but the fact that they accepted by faith what the Lord said regarding the lamb and its shed blood. Salvation by faith in the promises of God.

Propitiation (or Satisfaction). The Lord entered Egypt in judgment (Exod. 12:12), but the sight of the blood caused him to pass over the houses of Israel in peace. This is what the Bible knows as 'propitiation' (the allaying of wrath; the soothing away of anger). In a word, the holy God is satisfied regarding those who take refuge under the shed blood; he finds no case against them; he passes over in peace.

Equivalence (or Substitution). The selection of the Passover Lamb was made on a carefully worded prospectus (Exod. 12:3–5). It had to be 'according to the number of the persons', and 'according to each man's need' (lit., each person's eating, Exod. 12:4)—equivalent to number and need. To start with, this was an estimate, but, after passover night, any remainder of the lamb was consumed by fire, (v. 10), i.e., the lamb was thus made to be the exact equivalent of those who took shelter under its shed blood. But the relationship was also more intimate than merely numerical: when verse 30 says 'there was not a house where there was not one dead' it spoke the truth, except that in the blood-marked houses it was the dead body, not of the firstborn but of the lamb! Does this mean that the lamb saved only the firstborn? Look back to Exodus 4:22, 'Israel is my son, my firstborn.' The Lord looked on the whole people he intended to save as his 'firstborn': for them the lamb was the exact equivalent, and in their place the lamb died. Exodus 12:5 simply requires that 'your lamb shall be without blemish' (lit. 'perfect'), but throughout Leviticus (1:4; etc.,) and thereafter it becomes clear that this requirement is deeply important: only the perfect can bear the sins of another.

Salvation was (not simply made possible but) actually accomplished on Passover night. Before Passover they could not leave Egypt; after Passover they could not stay (Exod. 11:1). Before Passover they were a slave people, helpless and hopeless, under an edict of extermination (Exod. 1:22); at Passover they became a pilgrim people, dressed for the road (Exod. 12:11), a people liberated to walk with God.

ISRAEL AT SINAI

The People set out from Egypt to go to the promised land of Canaan, but they travelled rather to Mt. Sinai. It was not that they mistook the road, or (as we might say 'got their guidance wrong'). There was no possibility of a mistake;

the great Pillar of Cloud and Fire (Exod. 13:21–22) saw to that! Sinai was an essential destination because (as we saw above) those who had been redeemed by the blood of the lamb must now be instructed in the way of obedience. It is because they have been redeemed that they must hear the voice of the law (Exod. 20:2).

At Sinai, however, two other characteristic components of Israel's life came together: the Tabernacle and the Sacrifices.

The Tabernacle

The importance of the Tabernacle is indicated in the amount of space given to it in the Bible: first (Exod. 25–31) the materials, measurements, furnishings and personnel of the Tabernacle are spelled out in detail; then (Exod. 36–40) the same details are repeated, but this time describing the way they were constructed and put in place. We might well ask why such detail, and why twice over! The answer is given in Exodus 29:42–5. Far from being needlessly repetitious, the Tabernacle is the very reason why the Lord brought his people out of Egypt. To put it another way: the Tabernacle is the very purpose achieved by redemption through the blood of the lamb—'that I may dwell among them'. The beautiful and ornate Tent had a simple, specific purpose: they were a tent-dwelling people, and the Lord wished to dwell among them, and would have his Tent at the centre of theirs, as Numbers 2 shows, so that he could live among his people.

The Sacrifices

So, then, at the centre of the camp lay the Tabernacle, marked out by the overshadowing Cloud (Exod. 40:34), as the actual place where God himself lived. But at once they discovered that this was peril as well as privilege. Moses could not enter because God was there in all his glory (Exod. 40:35), and it is a repeated emphasis in the ceremonial law that death was the penalty of any and every trespass upon the divine presence (e.g., Lev. 8:35; 15:31). The awesome holiness of Sinai (Exod. 19:12; cf., Heb. 12:20) was matched by the holiness of the Lord's Tent (Exod. 29:43; 30:25–9). But, following the incident of the Golden Calf and the broken Law (Exod. 32), the people at last realised their state as sinners and the perils of sin (Exod. 33:4–6). The question therefore became crucial: how can sinners dwell with and approach a holy God? It was to meet this problem that the Lord provided the sacrifices.

Within the complexity of the sacrificial code, there were three main offerings:

1. The Burnt Offering represented, for the offerer, 'holding nothing back' from the Lord (cf., Gen. 22:2,12). In the burnt offering (Lev. 1) 'the whole' (vv. 9, 13 RV) was 'sent up' by fire to the Lord.
2. The Peace Offering (Lev. 3) represented, not making, but enjoying peace with God. Strikingly there is no reference to atonement in Leviticus 3. The peace offering was an occasion of family and wider fellowship in the accompanying meal (Lev. 7:15–20;

Deut.12:7,18). Peace horizontally as well as vertically; peace with others as well as with God.

3. The Sin Offering (Lev. 4) was designed to deal with sin, and the details offered in Leviticus 4 major on the themes of atonement and purification and on the ritual of the sprinkling of the blood.

'Atonement' throughout Leviticus 1–4 expresses the idea of 'covering' which we have already noted—the payment of the 'covering price'. This is a feature of the Burnt Offering (Lev. 1:4) as well as the Sin Offering (4:20, 26). There is, however, an important rite common to all three offerings: the laying of the worshipper's hand on the head of the sacrificial beast (1:4; 3:28, 13; 4:4, 15, 24). This act is explained in the Day of Atonement ritual where, acting on behalf of the whole congregation, Aaron lays his hands on the head of the goat, confessing over it all the transgressions, iniquities and sins of the people, 'putting them on the head of the goat', about which Leviticus says that it 'shall bear on itself all their iniquities' (Lev. 16:21–22). The laying on of the hand was thus both a gesture identifying the beast with the worshipper, and (where appropriate) a gesture of impartation, relieving the worshipper of anything that might stand between him and God, laying the need on the beast.

SUBSTITUTION

No examination of the Passover Event which takes the recorded details into serious account can end other than in affirming a substitutionary relationship between the selected lamb and Israel, God's firstborn. It is the same with the sacrifices. The rite of the laying on of the hand demands that this beast is now thought to stand before God in the place of the offerer—whether representing offerers in their 'ideal' of holding nothing back in consecration, or entering fully into divine fellowship, or as a sinbearer in their place.

Furthermore, the animal did all this in a real and effective sense. The sin offering, for example, was not provided as a picture of dealing with sin but as the reality: 'So the priest shall make atonement for them, and it shall be forgiven them' (7:20). Imagine a husband and wife in conversation. The husband comes home after a visit to the Tabernacle or Temple.

Husband: How wonderful to have ones sins forgiven!

Wife: How do you know your sins have been forgiven?

Husband: I saw the appointed animal die in my place, paying my price.

Wife: But how do you know your sins are forgiven?

Husband: Because, as taught, I laid my hand on its head, appointing it as my substitute.

Wife: Nevertheless, how do you know your sins are forgiven?

Husband: Because the Lord himself says so!

In other words, the Old Testament believer stood in exactly the same position as does the Christian believer today: 'Just as I am thou wilt receive/ wilt welcome, pardon, cleanse, relieve/ because thy promise I believe/ O Lamb of God, I come.' To see this to be true of our Old

Testament ancestors, we need only recall the opening of Psalm 51 with which this chapter began. On the basis of a hyssop-sprinkling of blood, there was the reality of grace, love, blotting out, washing and cleansing.

THE BLOOD OF BULLS AND GOATS

A very important question arises here, and one which lies at the heart of the cumulative revelation which the Bible presents. If the Old Testament sacrifices did actually secure the benefits associated with them, how can Hebrews (10:4) say that 'it is impossible for the blood of bulls and goats to take away sin'?

Leviticus 17:11 is a clear statement of the main Old Testament position.

It starts with a statement of the obvious: that flesh and blood, as long as they stay together constitute life. We are probably intended to draw the implicit conclusion: that either, in isolation from the other, is an indication that death has taken place.

Secondly, the verse teaches that the sacrificial system is a gift of God; his plan and provision, not a human expedient, or a human contrivance to put pressure on God. The sacrifices are his gracious idea and provision.

The divine purpose in the sacrifices is that the blood—the visible sign of life terminated—provides the atonement or covering price 'for' the soul (the object to which the atonement is applied). Finally, in additional explanation, with a change of preposition in the Hebrew, the blood makes this atonement (pays this covering price) (either or both) at the expense of the soul (the animal life laid down), or in the place of the soul (the life of the sinner which otherwise would be forfeit).

Was there an advance on this position when David, in Psalm 51:7, discerned a grace in God, a hyssop sprinkling, beyond what the levitical sacrifices provided? Possibly so, but the really new and vital perception came with Isaiah when, in 52:13–53:12, he foresaw the Servant of the Lord 'wounded because of our transgressions' when 'the Lord laid on him the iniquity of us all' (53:5–6). Isaiah used the time honoured terminology of the sacrifices, but he saw that ultimately it was necessary that a human become the substitutionary sacrifice—that only another human could be the true substitute for humans. Isaiah did in fact see the reason for this, but we will turn to Hebrews 10 to see it worked out and applied. Animals can perfectly depict substitution, their bodies the material for sacrifice; their 'innocent perfection' taking the place of my sinful being. But looking back, it can only be a picture, not the full reality, because the animal has no consenting will to match my will, which is the very ground-spring of my sinfulness. Animal sacrifices leave the sinner without a substitute where a substitute is most needed. Jesus, however, says Hebrews 10:7, comes into the world with the commitment, 'Behold, I have come…to do your will, O God,' and, for emphasis, it is repeated in verse 9, 'Behold, I have come to do your will.' Hence, Jesus is the 'one sacrifice for sins for ever' (Heb. 10:12). God's age-long plan of substitutionary salvation has at last been given perfect expression, accomplishment, and finality.

11

THE GREAT UNITIES:

ONE STORY, ONE MESSIAH

The Old Testament is full of wonderful, gripping, exciting stories—and I was fortunate enough to enjoy them (along with stories from the Gospels) every childhood bed-time. It is, of course, a much deeper matter than merely 'good stories'—thankful though we should be for that. The stories have the important function of carrying forward the ongoing salvation-history, from its first announcement in Genesis 3:15 to the fullness of time (Gal. 4:4) and the birth and saving work of Jesus. In this salvation-history, kingship came to play a leading part.

BAD IDEA, BEST IDEA

When the people first asked Samuel to find them a king (1 Sam. 8), they were, of course, opting for something less than the highest. Samuel plainly felt that the people were rejecting the institution of Judgeship, with an implied reflection on himself, but the Lord brought the issue to its proper point: 'they have not rejected you, but they have rejected me, that I should not reign over them' (1 Sam. 8:7). The system of Judgeship demanded faith— trusting that when a national crisis arose the Lord would have a deliverer at hand (Judges 2:18). How much more comfortable, they thought, to have a king, a permanent, ready-made deliverer should a crisis arise! But there is such mercy in the Lord, that he turned their second best into his best messianic plan. His coming Messiah would be a King, yes, and in the succession of the king they sinfully desired! Herein is the grace and the wonder of divine sovereign Providence. To see this at work we must start with the Book of Judges—but, first, a reminder about the nature of history in the Old Testament.

HISTORY AND SELECTION

This illustration may sound frivolous, but it is seriously meant: I have yet to read a history of the twentieth century which mentions my grandmother! Now, if I were to write about the twentieth century, she would loom very largely in it. You see, historians start with a point of view, and on the basis of their point of view they select, out of all the facts that lie before them, those that measure up to their estimate of what is important. If their grandmothers were important, they would be 'in'; if they think the most important factors were prime ministers and generals, then they write a history focused on politics and warfare—and so on. If they are disenchanted with 'narrative history', they opt for social or economic statistics. Even historians who do not think that 'history' gives any evidence of a purpose being worked out, nevertheless are obliged to select what they record out of all the facts available to them.

This does not mean that 'history' has to be 'tendentious', i.e., twisted or adjusted to make it conform to the historian's presuppositions—it could be, of course, but it does not have to be: objectivity can be seen and secured even if there is a personal 'point of view' which governs selection. We rely on the integrity of the individual historian to make this possible. We expect historians to treat the facts as sacred.

In this spirit we approach the Bible histories. Their 'point of view' is well illustrated in the fact that the fifty-five year reign of Manasseh (2 Kgs. 21) merits only eighteen verses, and all we learn of him is that he did evil in the sight of the Lord (vv. 2, 9, 11, 16). That, you see, is the 'point of view' of the biblical historian; it is what Bible history sets out to explore; it is what is important; it is the basis of selection from all available (2 Kgs. 21:17) facts about Manasseh. This does not make it less than reliable history; it is simply history resting on different presuppositions—and no worse for that!

So then, back to the Book of Judges to discover what makes Bible historians 'tick'.

THE BOOK OF JUDGES

The Book of Judges is in three parts. Joshua records the wars of conquest, as Israel entered the Promised Land; Judges takes over by recounting some of the wars of occupation whereby Israel started settling in conquered territory. This was an uneven process, during which Joshua died. Then started the period of Israel's unfaithfulness (Judges 2:11), and the accompanying recurring acts of undeserved divine pity (2:15–18). Thus the pattern for the period of the Judges was set up: unfaithfulness, divine pity, the rising up of the Judge to deliver, followed, after the death of the judge, by further unfaithfulness.

It is for this reason that we speak of the judges, not only as great leaders but as great failures. As individuals they could hardly be more varied—do we think of the loveable Gideon, the little man from the small tribe who performed scintillating deeds, or the buffoon Samson who could never resist either a prank or a girl; the unknown Shamgar or the seemingly cold and punctilious rigorist, Jephthah? They could momentarily pull together the separated tribes into a unity, and temporarily bring oppression and subjugation to an end. They could give the land even eighty years peace, but, after that, the repeat menu of unfaithfulness and loss.

What a 'come-down', then, to read chapters 17–21! It is like entering a dark, dank cellar, with the pervasive smell of disorder and decay! But that is exactly what it is. The Book of Ruth, which also belongs to 'the days when the judges ruled' (1:1), records a different side to the picture, but, as we noted, every historian has his point of view, and here both are valid. The author of Judges sees a problem, and offers a solution. 'There was no king', but if there had been one…?

THE HUNT FOR THE MESSIAH

Picture Elkanah and Hannah, with the boy Samuel, on their way to Shiloh, to Eli and the Lord's Tent, for the boy's dedication to life-long service there. Imagine them planning the details of the Service of Dedication, and Hannah says, 'Oh, do let's sing, "My heart rejoices in the Lord"!' (1. Sam. 2:1–10). See how her chosen hymn ends: '…exalt the horn of his anointed.' It was not only the author of Judges who saw the ideal Israel as centred on an anointed king. Others did as well. In other words, with Judges in our hands, and Hannah's chosen hymn, we can see 1 Samuel 8:5 not as expressing the wish of a few activists, but as representing something of a groundswell of opinion. To call the envisaged king 'his anointed' not only reflected what was, doubtless, the customary rite of initiation (e.g., 1 Sam. 10:1) but indicates the beginning of the messianic understanding of kingship. From this

Read Psalm 2 in the light of this paragraph about kingship and expectation. Think of it as sung at the coronation of a new king in David's line, holding up before him all it is hoped he will be—including that he will be, in some special sense a son of God, and that he will bring in the world dominion promised to David (e.g., Ps. 89:20–29). Read Psalm 72 in the same light. It is ascribed to Solomon, and we can think of the king pondering the future, mediating on the son who is yet to come.

beginning grew the Books of Kings, as our ancestors in Israel fixed their eyes on the future, longed for the ultimate king, and pondered whether each new king in David's line could turn out to be the Lord's truly anointed.

THE SWINGING SPOT-LIGHT

We have to have our wits about us when we read 2 Kings, because it is written as a historical amalgam of two kingdoms. Rehoboam, who succeeded Solomon, was something of a nincompoop, and he was swayed by visions of grandeur ministered to him by his contemporary hotheads. He would be the one to put right his father's failures by strong, decisive, uncompromising action! And, as weak leaders do, he chose the wrong issue on which to make his decisive stand, the wrong time, and the wrong methods! All this resulted (1 Kings 12) in the irretrievable division of the kingdom into the tiny, two-tribe enclave of 'Judah' to the south, and the larger, ten-tribe nation of 'Israel' to the north. In these two sections two different types of kingship are to be seen.

In Judah the line of David continued, in orderly succession, father to son, from David (1000 BC) until the fall of Jerusalem (587 BC), kings within the Lord's covenant with David (2 Sam. 7), sitting on Yahweh's throne (1 Chr. 29:23)

In Israel the situation was different. The first king, Jeroboam, is introduced as a vigorous, thrustful adventurer, who reached the summit of his ambition on the throne of Israel (1 Kgs. 11:26–40; 12:25–14:20). He set the pattern. The kings of Israel were gifted, power-hungry individuals who, for the most part reached the throne by their personal efforts—strong, natural leaders, very few of whom founded even brief dynasties, many of whose reigns ended in assassination.

Two distinct types of kingship: the one, unelected, reaching the throne by inheritance; the other, the gifted man, climbing up by his own boot-straps. It is between these two 'poles' that the historian's spot-light swings. Will the ordered succession within David's covenant produce the Messiah? Or is he to be found on the basis of natural, human gift and ability?

The historian's answer is, 'Neither'. Israelite kingship was the first to go, drowned in the tide of Assyrian imperialistic advance in 722 BC (2 Kgs. 17). Judah followed one hundred and forty or so years later, this time overwhelmed by Babylonian imperialism, whereby, though the line of David continued (2 Kgs. 25:27–30), it disappeared under the sands of time only to emerge when he came whose right it is to reign (Luke 1:31–5).

THE MESSIANIC HOPE

Throughout the many years between the request for a king and the fall of Jerusalem, alongside the dismal record of royal failure, there arose and grew the expectation of the King Messiah. Many writers put forward the theory that it took the ultimate shock of the fall of Jerusalem and the destruction of the throne of David to kick-start the expectation of the coming true King. This, of course, runs contrary to the fact that the great hope is expressed so frequently by the pre-exilic prophets, and leads to the necessity of re-ordering and re-dating much of the Bible. But the theory is unnecessary. Monarchy was a failure from the start; the golden expectations of Judges 17–21 largely unfulfilled. If prior disappointment is a necessary preliminary to the growth of hope, it was there in full and plenty right from the beginning. Saul failed to unite the nation; David pioneered moral collapse; Solomon gave a lead to religious corruption; and the break between 'Judah' and Israel frustrated the scintillating and truly miraculous forecasts of the Messiah to come.

David continued to hold a central position as the golden king (1 Kgs. 11:4; 15:11). Messiah will sit on David's throne (Isa. 9:7); when Isaiah envisages the saving work of the Servant of the Lord (Isa. 52:13–53:12), he implies (55:3) that this is the fulfilment of 'the sure mercies of David'. To Jeremiah, Messiah is a 'Branch' (in a family tree) tracing his ancestry to David (Jer. 23:5). In Ezekiel 34 (v. 24) it will be like David himself come back as the perfect Shepherd of the Lord's flock.

King and Priest. Zechariah foresaw the coming of 'The Branch' (which must have become, by his time, a conventional title of Messiah, arising from the prophecies of Isaiah and Jeremiah) as an enthroned priest (Zech. 6:12–13). The central text on this theme is Psalm 110, where we meet with David meditating on the royal messianic hope established in his dynasty. So great is this coming One that even David calls him 'Lord' (cf., Matt. 22:43), and not only so but, parallel to the divine word appointing Messiah to his royal state (110:1), there is a divine oath (110:4) that he will be an eternal Priest in the line of Melchizedek (cf., Heb.

5:9–10; 7:1–28). Melchizedek first appears in the Bible in Genesis 14. Abram was returning from his defeat of the kings of the earth, and, when Melchizedek came out to meet him, he responded by giving him a tithe of all the spoils he had amassed (v. 20). This meant that Abram (the king of kings) acknowledged Melchizedek as his superior. Abram went on to identify Melchizedek's God ('God Most High') as the true god, Yahweh (v. 22), and thus to acknowledge Melchizedek's priesthood as a true priesthood. Hundreds of years later, when Joshua was conquering the Promised Land, the king of Jerusalem was one, 'Adoni-zedek' (Josh. 10:1), a name of exactly the same form and meaning as Melchizedek! 'Melchi' means 'king of' and 'Adoni' means 'Sovereign of'. Is it too great a leap of imagination to think that the same royal line survived in Jerusalem—and with it the same royal priesthood? I think not. But the consequence is that when David set up his throne in Jerusalem (2 Sam. 5:6–10), he, in turn, became the Melchizedek Priest—a separate priesthood (cf., Heb. 7:14–19) resident in the royal house—and, according to Psalm 110, one of the special ways in which the royal Messiah to come was understood.

The Messianic enigma arises when we note that the Messiah is also 'the branch of the Lord', i.e., tracing his ancestry to the Lord; Messiah is born as a human baby (Isa. 9:6) to inherit David's throne, and fulfil David's promises (9:7), born within David's line, yet his names (9:6) include 'mighty God'- the very words 10:21 uses of Yahweh himself! This dual relationship comes again in Isaiah: in 53:2–4 the Servant of the Lord is plainly a man among men, with earthly origin and earthly appearance. But he is also 'the arm of the Lord' (53:1), i.e., the Lord himself with his sleeves rolled up for action (cf., 52:10). When Jeremiah (23:6) foresees Messiah as David's Branch, he also says his name is 'The Lord our righteousness'. The Old Testament does not explain how a human Messiah can also be divine. It does, however, insist that he is a supernatural person in his birth of a virgin (Isa. 7:14): the birth as such was human, but the infant born was 'God with us'. In Malachi (3:1) it was the Lord himself who was to come.

The Suffering Messiah. David does not supply us with any background to Psalm 22. We do know, of course, that Jesus applied it to himself as the crucified Messiah (Mark 15:34), and we can only assume that in the course of some life-threatening and dire suffering that came to him, David was enabled to foresee the Suffering King yet to come. It fell to Isaiah to work this theme out in his portrayal of the Suffering Servant of the Lord—the Messiah who would bring revealed truth to the Gentile world (Isa. 42:1–4), who would bring errant Israel back to the Lord (49:1–6), who, at fearful cost, would live out the life of obedience (50:4–9), and who would be 'wounded for our transgressions' (52:13–53:12).

Even though we are able only to take our review to this point, what a rich forecast the Old Testament offers— and what a remarkable book that, so far in advance, it so perfectly detailed what was yet to come!

Other references to pursue in building up the prediction of the Messiah: Ps. 2; Dan. 7; Amos 9:11–15; Mic. 5:2–5a; Zech. 6:12–13; Mal. 3:1; 4:5–6.

12

PRACTICALITIES: PROPHETS AND PSALMS

The Word of God says:

Of this salvation the prophets have enquired and searched diligently. They prophesied of the grace that would come to you. Searching what or what manner of time the Spirit of Christ who was in them was indicating when he testified beforehand of the sufferings of the Messiah and the glories that would follow. To them it was revealed that not themselves but to us they were ministering the things that have now been reported to you through those who have preached the Gospel to you by the Holy Spirit sent down from heaven—things which angels desire to look into.'

(1 Peter 1:10–12)

We all need lots of help—and determination—if we are to become familiar with the books of the prophets. There are so many of them! And, at first sight, it all looks so daunting—acres of print, just one thing after another, words without excitement! Possibly it would stimulate our motivation if we were to recall that in their day the prophets were the headline makers: to the 'establishment' of his day, Amos was a nationally known trouble-maker, to the extent that he was threatened with a deportation order (Amos 7:10–13); Isaiah hired hoarding space to write up a slogan to catch the eye of the passer-by (30:8a); Ezekiel was a master of the visual aid—even breaking through the wall of his own house (12:4–7)! The prophets were the talking point of their time, and it may be our fault rather than theirs if we find their books dull.

READ...RE-READ...AND READ AGAIN...AND AGAIN

The initial help we need lies to hand in the shape of *The New Bible Commentary*, 21st Century Edition (IVP, 1994). It provides a brief, useful introduction to each of the books of the Bible in turn, and a helpful companion as we read through. But—and we must face it—there is no alternative to the reading and re-reading which builds up layer upon layer of knowledge of what is there in each of the prophets, and which gradually lets us see the structure or pattern of each book. To a large extent we find the books of the prophets unattractive because they are unfamiliar: we have not taken the trouble or the discipline of getting to know them. We will return to this topic presently, but it is so important that it has to be emphasised at once: nothing can take the place of reading…re-reading…reading again…and again… It is only when we engage in repeated reading that the books of the prophets begin to yield up their structure to us, and begin to let us into their meaning (and excitement).

MALACHI

The book of Malachi is an encouraging place to start because he makes the structure of his book so plain, and in this way breaks it down into manageable sections. I find it helpful to imagine Malachi as an open-air preacher, with a loyal company of persistent hecklers. Whatever subject he opens up, they have a counter proposition to make! Finally, Malachi decides to use their heckling as the best way to record his ministry and message.

The following outline of Malachi shows the two main stages of reading and studying the prophets. The first represents stage one or the initial target: to expose what is there—so that Malachi is no longer just a blur of print, but a list of topics; the second goes further, probing the contents of the list to see if the items listed are part of a more balanced pattern. We might well want to ask if Malachi deliberately planned that the second and fifth of his questions should be asked in a double form. Probably not, but we are dealing also with the mind of the Holy Spirit who inspired Malachi, and it would seem from the evidence of the Bible that he loves this sort of balance and symmetry.

Malachi in Outline

Topics Malachi proposed and questions he was asked

1:2	How can we believe in a God of love?
1:6	What have I ever done to offend God?
2:14	Why doesn't God answer prayers?
2:17	Is there such a thing as 'good'?
3:7–8	What do I have to give up?
3:14	Is it worth while being religious?

I have tried to express the 'heart' or principle at issue in Malachi's questions. Judge for yourself.

Malachi's questions seen as a pattern

God's Love (1:1–5). Looking around at events and experiences, it is easy to deny a God of love, difficult always to discern one. The Lord points to the future: take the long view.

(Double Question). Cheap Religion (1:6–2:9). Dealing with God on the level of the second best.

Behaviour (2:10–16). The particular matter of the marriage covenant and fidelity to promises.

Behaviour (2:17–3:6). The basic issue of moral values and of living by God's standards—which he will ultimately vindicate and enforce.

(Double Question). Cheap Religion (3:7–12). Responding obediently to God's requirements is the way of blessing.

God's Love (3:13–4:6). The heckler questions the worthwhileness of responding to God's laws; the Lord reveals present realties (v. 16) and future prospects (vv. 17–4:6).

AMOS

Amos presents a slightly more complicated problem of analysis, but, again, one which yields up its secret to persevering reading. In Amos 1:2 Amos uses the metaphor of a roaring lion—the verb 'roar' is specifically the pouncing roar of a lion, about to savage its prey. The same picture reappears in 3:8. This could be what is called an 'inclusion', i.e., matching thoughts acting as brackets around a section. It offers us a clue worth pursuing. Amos 3:9–11 turns from metaphor to reality, an enemy 'all round the land', and, reading forward, we find the same thought at 6:11—a hostile force attacking both north ('the entrance of Hamath') and south ('the valley of the Arabah'), where the north/south contrast is an idiom for 'everywhere'. In 7:1–6 Amos envisages a plague of locusts and a fire, either of which would spell the end of the nation. He prays against them and the Lord promises 'it shall not be.' If we describe this as a doom that will not happen, then it is an inclusion by contrast with 9:11–15 as a hope that will happen. In this way the book of Amos breaks down into three manageable sections, each of which is capable of analysis as the accompanying diagram shows.

As the diagrams show, the task of analysing content can be carried beyond simply marking off the main sections: each section is itself capable of analysis. But, to return to the basic task, when the main sections of a book (or psalm) have been identified, the next step is to describe the content of each section, and, in this way, to gain a grasp of what—in this case, Amos—is about.

Section 1 consists of a parade of the nations, starting with the surrounding heathen nations (1:2–2:3), and leading up to the two nations of the Lord's people (2:4–3:8). There is one God to whom the whole world is accountable, and who will call the nations to account. He has observed the whole course of their offensiveness: the recurring formula 'for three rebellions and for four' speaks of divine watchfulness and patience; no rush to judgment; ample periods of probation; but then, the 'fourth rebellion' came and, so to speak, made the onset of judgment inevitable. Amos is, however, very precise in isolating the cause of divine judgment in each case. In the case of the nations who never knew the special grace of divine revelation, judgment is pronounced on 'crimes against humanity', the offended voice of conscience; in the case of Judah and Israel, the unforgiveable, fourth rebellion, was rejecting the Lord's Word (2:4), silencing the voice of special revelation (2:4, 11–12).

The central truth in section two is the Lord's control of all the events of history, his mastery of the nations, in the interests of his own moral purposes, and, in particular his use of the events of history when his people need chastisement and correction. The core of the section in chapters 4 and 5 teaches us that, when faced with circumstantial adversity our first thought should be to make sure that we are right with God—the call, five times over, to 'return to the Lord' in verses 6–11; parallel to this, in chapter 5, is the reminder that religious punctiliousness is no replacement for moral reformation and godly living. The Lord is not impressed by ritualism, as such.

What would we do without the last section of Amos? Our theology would be truncated indeed. Amos has majored on judgment to the extent that even our privileged position (3:1–2) makes us all the more culpable, but it is impossible to be a prophet of Yahweh and not have a message of hope. Yahweh is the God who saves his

Amos in Outline

1:1   Title

1:2–3:8   The Lion's Roar: Universal Judgment and its grounds

       1:2 The Lion's roar: the Lord's Voice (A)
       1:3–2:3 Against the pagan peoples (B)
       2:4–3:2 Against the chosen people (B)
       3:3–8 The Lion's roar: the prophetic Word (A)

3:9–6:14 An Enemy around the Land: the Lord's Anger

       3:9–15 The Shattered Kingdom (A)
       4:1–3 The Leading Women (B)
       4:4–13 Religion without Repentance (C)
       5:1–27 Religion without Reformation (C)
       6:1–7 The Leading Men (B)
       6:8–14 The Shattered Kingdom (A)

7:1–9:15 The Lord God: Judgment and Hope

       7:1–6 The Devastation that will not be (A)
       7:7–9 Discriminating Judgment (B)
       7:10–17 The Inescapable Word (C)
       8:1–14 'In that Day' (D)
       9:1–6 The Inescapable Judgment (C)
       9:7–10 Discriminating Judgment (B)
       9:11–15 The Hope that will be (A)

people as well as overthrows his foes: such is the Exodus revelation, and, faithful to it, Amos ends his book with 'the hope that shall be', the fulfilment of the promises to David (9:11–12) and, in effect, the new heaven and new earth (9:13–15).

ISAIAH

Unfamiliarity is the enemy of understanding the prophets of the Old Testament; committed reading and re-reading is the only way forward, and, as we will now see, it works with the immensely long 'major prophets' as well—it just takes more time!

The most obvious suggestion, when one starts to read Isaiah, is that, since his call to be a prophet comes at what to us is chapter 6, chapters 1–5 are probably intended as a 'preface' to the whole book: setting the scene for the recorded prophecies that are to follow.

The next section is marked of by our old friend the 'inclusion': chapter 6 records how one sinner found salvation; chapter 12 describes a whole community drawing from the wells of salvation.

Next come three sub-sections of fives: the first two (13–20, 21–23) are given titles by Isaiah; the third sub-section (24–27), on examination, also proves to be five-fold, but it has no headings. It is as if Isaiah is probing forward from the shape of the world he knows (13–20) into a 'hazier' future (21–23) where he uses 'cryptic' titles, and finally into the future of the end time (24–27) where two cities are seen in tension: the global city of human attempts to create a world that is at one—but which Isaiah calls 'the city of confusion' (24:10), and the 'strong city' of salvation (26:1) in which those who trust Yahweh are safe.

Moving on, Isaiah divides up his next section (chs. 28–35) by using the summoning word 'Woe' six times (28:1; 29:1; 29:15; 30:1; 31;1; 33:1).

Chapters 36–39 consist of two historical 'panels': Chapters 36–37 look back to what has just been covered in Isaiah's ministry, and records the overthrow of the Assyrian forces by the Lord's Angel (37:36); chapters 38–39 look forward, recounting Hezekiah's cardinal sin, and predicting exile in Babylon.

In chapters 40–48 Isaiah envisages his people in Babylon and predicts their return home, but, cf. 48:20–22, they return with the problem of sin, and reconciliation with the Lord, still unresolved.

This is the task now given to 'the Servant of the Lord' (49:5), alongside his role as 'salvation to the ends of the earth' (49:6). That this double task is actually performed by the Servant's substitutionary death (52:12–53:12) is heralded by the double call—chapter 54, to Zion; chapter 55, to the world—to enter into freely offered free salvation.

The final chapters (56–66) envisage the Lord's people still awaiting salvation (56:1), which, at first sounds strange, as if the atoning work of Isaiah 53 left anything undone! Then we recall that this is exactly how we are placed: Jesus has indeed offered one sacrifice for sins for ever (Heb. 10:12), yet we too still await the consummation of that salvation when he comes again. Isaiah foresees this as the advent and work of an anointed Conqueror (59:20–21; 61:1–3; 61:10–62:7; 63:1–6), issuing in the new heaven and new earth (65: 17–25).

Space forbids pursuing the content of Isaiah any further, but, please God, enough may have been included to whet your appetite for the joyful task of reading and re-reading God's word until it yields up its secrets.

PSALMS

More than any other part of the Old Testament, the Psalms repay reading and re-reading, leading to analysis. They are after all, the planned products of outstandingly gifted (not to mention divinely inspired) poets. Like Paul's epistles they hold together the outpourings of the heart and the well-thought-out intentions of the mind, and we should expect to be able to discover the structures and plans through which the poet (under the inspiration of the Holy Spirit) expressed his thought.

A Central Thought

One general observation is worth making before we launch into some examples of Psalm structure. The Psalms are not only the longest book of the Bible; they are also the most varied. All life, in all its variety and complexity, is represented here. Yet all this multiplicity can be brought under one heading: 'take it to the Lord.' You know how you can take a mirror and so angle it to the sun that sunlight can be re-directed into a dark corner—

or wherever? The Psalms teach us to set our lives at an angle, making sure our lives are so 'angled' that everything is at once transmitted into the Lord's presence, and put into the context of what is true about him.

Would an illustration help? Growing up in Dublin, our school atlases naturally had a map of Ireland on page one. Later there was a map of Australia on the same sized page! To avoid misunderstanding, in the bottom right hand corner of the Australia page there was a tiny, postage-stamp-sized map entitled 'Ireland on the same scale'. Thus things were to be seen in their proper proportions! The two countries could be displayed on the same sized page but they were far from being of the same size! Now suppose the editors had decided to achieve the same result in a different way, suppose they had decided to attach to the Ireland page a map of Australia on the same scale—a map which opened up fold upon fold upon fold upon fold, its immensity dwarfing Ireland's comparative minuteness! At any rate, this is exactly what Psalms do: they put their undeviating understanding of the greatness of the Lord alongside our situations, so that we may have a due sense of the correct proportion of things. The lovely old song says 'Turn your eyes upon Jesus; look full in his wonderful face; and the things of earth will grow strangely dim, in the light of his glory and grace'—'Grow strangely dim', i.e., be seen in their true colours and perspective. This is exactly the function the Psalms fulfil as they teach us to take everything to the Lord: Psalm 88 shows how even the direst trouble takes a new shape (without for a moment ceasing to be the direst

trouble) when we see 'God on the same scale'! Psalms 105
and 106 do the same for the contrasting experiences of
the course of history.

Psalm 124

Look at the outline offered of Psalm 124. Attentive reading shows that the 'frame' of the psalm is provided by
three assertions about the Lord in verses 1–2, 6a, 8—

Psalm 124	respectively the Lord is on our side
The LORD	(vv. 1–2), the Lord has been our deliv-
Earthquake	erer (v. 6a), and the Lord is our help
Flood	(v. 8)—the first and last being state-
The LORD	ments of unchanging fact, the second a
	recollection of a particular deliverance.
Beast of prey	In between this frame are pictorial rep-
Hunter	resentations of the dangers in which the
The LORD	Lord's presence and deliverance have
	been proved: verse 3, earthquake (such

as Num. 16:31–2); verses 4–5, flood waters; verse 6b, the
ravenous beast; verse 7, the hunter with his snare. The
psalm ends on a high note: not only is the danger over,
but it cannot recur: the snare itself is broken!

Psalm 100

Psalm 100 offers a comparable plan. In effect there are
two 'statements' about the Lord: verse 3 'He is God',
and verse 5a, he 'is good'. Each is followed by two
'amplifications': verse 3, 'he made us…we are his people',

verse 5, 'His mercy is everlasting…his truth endures…'; and each is preceded by a threefold call to approach and worship, in verse 1 'shout…serve…come'; and in verse 4, 'enter…be thankful…bless…'. Psalm 100 is particularly clear in demonstrating that once we see structure we see meaning and intention.

Psalm 121

Psalm 121 is an interesting study. First, there is one word which comes six times—though, sadly, even NKJV messes this up so that we have 'keep' in verses 3, 4 and 5 and 'preserve' in verses 7 and 8. (See RV and ESV for 'keep' throughout). There can be no doubt what the subject of the Psalm is—the 'keeping Lord'. But to take the thought of being 'kept' further we have to mark the points at which the emphasis changes. In verses 1–2 the Lord is God the Creator; in verses 3–4 there is an unexpected reference to 'Israel' as the object of divine keeping. 'Israel' is the name of the corporate first-born son redeemed by the blood of the lamb (Exod. 4:22), so that we are now thinking of God the Redeemer. In verses 5–6, however, the keeping Lord is our Companion, alongside, standing between us and the real danger from the sun, and the imagined danger from the moon—i.e., all dangers, whether of circumstances or imaginations. This threefold theology of Creator, Redeemer and Companion, then leads into the climax (vv. 7–8), keeping from all evil (7a), the whole person (7b), in every activity (8a), and for all time, starting now (8b).

More examples of psalm-structure can be studied in A. Motyer, 'Psalms', in New Bible Commentary, 21st Century Edition, IVP, 1994. See the same book for further information on Alphabets and Imprecations.

Alphabets and Imprecations

Alphabetic Psalms take the letters of the Hebrew Alphabet in turn as the opening letters of successive verses. The 'queen' of all alphabetic psalms is 119 where each letter is allocated eight verses, all referring, under different titles, to 'the word of God'. Though this sounds a formal and even artificial poetic style, it serves a deeper purpose. Just as in English usage an 'A to Z' covers every aspect of its subject, so also the 'aleph to tau' of Hebrew. Thus, Psalm 119 says to us: here is everything you need to know about the word of God. Where the alphabet is incomplete, commentators and even translators often seek to 'correct what is amiss and supply what is lacking' (as, e.g., NIV in Psalm 145:13). I believe this is a mistake, misunderstanding the significance of the alphabetic form. Sometimes the alphabet is left incomplete because the topic itself is inexhaustible. This is, I believe, the case with Psalm 145: who ever could exhaust the praises of God? In Psalms 9–10 the broken alphabet reflects the brokenness of life itself; likewise Psalm 34. This suggestion matches the nature of Hebrew Poetry where the poet's meaning dominates everything, and the form is used flexibly, adapted to the occasion.

There are quite a number of places in the Psalms where we find ourselves shocked by the thoughts expressed in the form of curses invoked upon other people. These are called the 'imprecatory psalms', with, say, 69 and 109 as outstanding examples of the genre. Very often commentaries simply dismiss the imprecations as examples of 'Old Testament morality', exposed and condemned by the higher revelation of God in Christ. This, however, is simply loose thinking. Psalm 139 is typical of many of the psalms which contain 'imprecations' in that it also contains clear evidence of a high theology, and an exalted spirituality of which honesty compels us to stand in awe. The Imprecatory Psalms are too big a subject to do anything more here than offer some pointers towards understanding them.

First, all the 'imprecations' are couched as prayers addressed to the Lord. They are not curses hurled at the heads of enemies. They are yet another aspect of 'take it to the Lord'—take it to the Lord and leave it there! (cf., Rom. 12:19).

Next, they are only and solely prayers, not a concealed plan of action. We would be wrong to draw any sort of conclusion—that they are prayers preparatory to the sort of retaliation which the Old Testament expressly forbids (Lev. 19:17–18). Nor should we assume that the psalmists, in framing imprecatory prayers, were indulging in the same feelings of vengefulness and animosity which might well be the case were I (or, maybe, you) to voice such thoughts. To ascribe a mind of sinful hatred to David when he penned Psalm 139 would be completely unwarranted. The imprecations express an anger that sins not (Eph. 4:26).

The problem set by Psalm 137:8–9 (a statement, not an imprecation) is one of translation. Study 'happy' (NKJV), 'blessed' (ESV) in a concordance. The Hebrew word (ashrey) according to context, can mean 'blessed' (under the blessing of God), 'happy' (fulfilled, contented), or 'right' (doing the right thing in a given situation). It is the last meaning that suits Psalm 137—not that it describes a thing right in itself but something 'right' in a world of moral reward.

Thirdly, read Deuteronomy 19:15–21. When a malicious accusation was made and proved false, the Law of God decreed that the offender be punished by the infliction of whatever he had thought to bring down on the one he falsely accused. The imprecations express this principle of equal justice, and ask for its implementation.

A Closer Walk with God

The words are the opening prayer of William Cowper's lovely hymn 'O for a closer walk with God'. Do they not chime in with the deepest desire of every child of God? There is no more practical way of helping them to become true than to immerse ourselves in the Psalms.

13

OVER THE BRIDGE

The Old Testament offers two main evidences that its God, Yahweh, is the only God: the work of creation, and the fulfilment of predictive prophecy. Psalm 96:5 is typical of the former: 'For all the gods of the peoples are no-gods, but it is Yahweh who made the heavens.' The Hebrew for 'gods' here is elohim, and 'no-gods' represents the punning word 'elilim.—sham efforts trying to ape the real thing that should deceive nobody! Whereas (if we are to catch the emphasis the Hebrew intends), 'it was actually the heavens Yahweh made.' As though to say, 'beat that if you can!'

ISAIAH'S TEACHING

The argument from fulfilled prediction is a speciality of Isaiah. In chapters 40–48 he envisages his people gone captive to Babylon, but predicts their surprising deliverance and return home. He foresaw it happening this way: a fresh conqueror, sweeping all before him, is on his way (41:2–4), raised up by Yahweh. Logically, this would be bad news for a captive people: they were helpless enough before Babylonian power; what price a mightier conqueror? 'Not to worry' counsels Isaiah, because this mightier conqueror is Yahweh's plan, indeed his 'anointed' (45:1), that is to say, equipped and empowered for a task Yahweh has imposed on him, namely to send the exiles home, and rebuild Yahweh's city (45:13). Yahweh even said, through his prophets, that were Cyrus to ponder events he could come to know that Yahweh is God (45:3), indeed, that anyone pondering events would reach the same conclusion (45:6). Please read Isaiah 44:21–45:13.

Of course, it looks as if things did not work out quite like that for Cyrus. When he arrived in Babylon all the priests were making the same claim for their particular god—that this or that 'god' was behind the fall of Babylon and the advent of Persia. Cyrus—like many another soldier turned politician, found himself obliged to exchange the sword in his hand for the tongue in his cheek! In the inscription known as the Cyrus Cylinder he ascribes his victories to Marduk, whereas in Ezra 1:2 he says it was Yahweh. All had won and all would have prizes. Nevertheless, Isaiah claimed, only one God was wise before the event; only Yahweh predicted and fulfilled his word; only Yahweh is God.

GODS IN CONTRAST

Isaiah's polemic for Yahweh as the only God, begins with the contrast drawn in 41:2–7. In verses 2–4 he foresees the uprising of a great conqueror (so far un-named), who has been raised by Yahweh; whose triumphant career has been superintended by Yahweh, and whose accomplishments are Yahweh's accomplishments. In other words, there is a God who initiates, controls, and determines the course of history: a God who, to make the point at issue, is wise before the event. Now, by contrast, look at the pagan situation (vv. 5–7): a frenzy of activity, rushing to 'make gods' under whose shelter they will be safe from the coming threat after it has arisen. 'Gods' only wise after the event; man-made expedients, as dead as the materials from which they have been created', things so inert (v. 7b) that they will topple over unless well secured with pegs!

Isaiah 41:1–7

- Invitation to make a case (v. 1).
- The question to be decided (v. 2–3).
- The God wise before the event (v. 4).
- The 'god' wise only after the event (v. 5–7).

See also Isaiah's great satirical exposé in 44:6–20. It is, of course, possible that to the more sophisticated pagan, thought would be directed past the material artefact to the 'spiritual' reality supposed to be represented by it, just as it might be easy to feel a sense of the numinous in the presence of some great idolatrous creation today. But, like the rest of the Old Testament, Isaiah will have none of this. To him, 'the heathen in their blindness bow down to wood and stone'. The only 'power' exercised by the idol is that we become like the god we worship (Isa.44:20; Ps.115:8).

THE CRUCIAL DIFFERENCE

Isaiah is at his most typical in 41:21–24. In these verses the Lord is challenging the false idol gods to prove their divine reality, and in this connection he proposes a test. Can they predict and then fulfil what they have predicted? Isaiah treats prophecy, prediction and fulfilment as seriously as that. It is the way in which a true God proves that he is the true God. So the Lord challenges the idols, 'Bring forth your strong reasons', i.e., this is a matter in which proof is possible, so, please, can we have your proofs? In verse 22, 'Let them bring forth and show us what will happen'—can they, in fact, predict?

Verse 22b calls for prediction by interpretation: It is possible to ponder what has already happened, to interpret the flow of events, and to discern their tendency and outcome. This is not necessarily a spiritual matter at

If, of course, as many today would have us believe, chapters 40–55 are the product of a 'second Isaiah' resident in Babylon contemporaneously with the events he spoke of, such a 'prophet' would never have dared use this argument from 'sheer prediction'—he would himself have been little more than a shrewd political commentator on current affairs! But consider how potent the argument from 'sheer prediction' is, when these chapters come from the remote, pre-exilic past! And what a reassuring comfort to the captive exiles!

all, but may be just evidence of cleverness, mental ability, a discernment and understanding of history. But it would still be prediction. Even at this level the idol gods fail.

Verses 22c–23a. With the words, 'Or declare to us things to come', Yahweh, through Isaiah, calls for sheer prediction: just say what is going to happen!

Isaiah's killing blow comes in mid-verse 23. The case against the idols runs beyond their inability to predict either by interpretation or by sheer foreknowledge. Just do anything whatever; show some vestige of activity; have a blank cheque to fill in as you please! The idols are as dead as their material representations.

Faithful to his depiction of a court case, with the idol-gods and Yahweh both producing evidence of their claim to deity, Isaiah allows us to hear the court's verdict. First, the idol-gods' (v. 24): as regards themselves, 'nothing'; as regards their alleged activity, 'nothing'. Their claim to deity is bogus and baseless, and there is no evidence to the contrary. But, then, as to Yahweh, he is Lord of history (v. 25); he initiates (v. 26a), and the verdict has to be in his favour: 'He is righteous/in the right'.

Such is Isaiah's claim for Yahweh. He was there at the start bringing into being the first moves in his historical purposes. The flow of history, so often to us a meaningless flux of

Isaiah 41:22–24

(a) The Proposed Topic
Predictive ability (v. 22a).
(b) Aspects of Prediction
  (i) The meaning and outcome of events (v. 22b).
  (ii) Absolute prediction (v. 22c).
(c) Significance
Proof of identity (v. 23).
(d) Conclusion
  (i) (v. 24).
  (ii) (v. 25–6).

actors, activities, movements and conflicts, is actually a closely guarded arena of divine purposes: the Lord is there in the flux, making sure that each event is in the right place at the right time, each 'actor' appears on cue, everything is perfectly integrated into the divine scheme, nothing intrusive retards or deflects the divine plan. And the God who was there at the start, who superintended the process, is there at the end to guarantee that what he willed and predicted happens in the fullness of his time (Gal. 4:4). Such a God is God indeed! Not only 'I am the first and I am the last' (44:6)—the eternal God, but 'I am the first and with the last' (41:4), the God of historical fulfilment and accomplishment, associated, at the end, with the predicted fruits of his sovereign management of people and affairs.

OVER THE BRIDGE

When we consider the abundance of Old Testament prediction fulfilled in the New Testament we need to take this thinking on board in a big way. What a great God is this! What a demonstration of divine reality, sovereignty and power! Can we ever ascribe a sufficiently exalted and all-embracing 'immensity' to such a God? A God who is God indeed!

In the New Testament we discover five notable avenues of fulfilment.

Obedience Fulfilment

The simplest (and greatest) way to illustrate this is to recall how the Lord Jesus 'found himself' in the Scriptures.

Luke, for example, chose to make the incident in 4:14–22 the point where Jesus' public ministry began, and he intended us to see verses 18–19 as Jesus' chosen manifesto. For our purpose the important thing to notice is that, when the Lord had read his chosen Scripture, he said, 'Today these words have been fulfilled in your hearing'. He found himself in the Old Testament Scriptures. He understood himself, and his role, his vocation, and his future from his Bible. He was content, later, to say: 'The Son of Man goes as it is written of him' (Matt. 26:24). The pathway was laid down in the Word of God, and he set himself to walk in it.

Matthew 26:51–4 is crucially important as an illustration of our Lord's determination to fulfil in himself what he perceived the Scriptures required of him.

The Lord Jesus has been arrested in the Garden, and Peter, Peter the bold, Peter the impulsive, drew his sword and sliced off the ear of the High Priest's servant. I cannot forebear to mention that this is the only totally just war that has ever been fought—and it fulfils all the requirements that supposedly go to the making of 'just war', but it is of this 'war' that the Lord Jesus, in principle, said, 'I will have nothing to do with it. So put your sword back into its sheath.' It is of this totally 'just war' that he said, 'They who take the sword will perish by the sword.' But enough of that. The crucial bit comes next: 'Do you think that I cannot now pray to my Father, and he will provide me with more than twelve legions of angels? How then could the Scripture be fulfilled, that it must happen thus?' Do you see how he tied himself to the Word of God? If we follow the Lord Jesus Christ, we are following the supreme Bible Man. Don't ever be ashamed of being thought of as being tied to Holy Scripture. Don't ever be ashamed of exalting Holy Scripture. You're following in the steps of Jesus who bound himself to the Word of God, and insisted by his obedience to fulfil what was written of him.

An equally telling and touching illustration of the Lord's 'obedience fulfilment' of prediction comes in John 19:28. On the Cross he said, 'I thirst.' Now I am told that dehydration, with excruciating thirst, is one of the torments of crucifixion. But, according to John, Jesus did not say 'I thirst' because he was thirsty, but 'in order that the Scripture might be fulfilled.' Dare we venture to think that on the cross he was searching his capacious memory—Have I really done everything that the Bible requires me to do? Have I really fulfilled every word of prediction that the Bible would require me to fulfil? And in the light of Psalm 22:15 he said 'I thirst' 'in order that the Scripture might be fulfilled'. The Lord Jesus found himself in Scripture, and set himself to fulfil its predictions by his obedience.

Circumstantial Fulfilment

Secondly, there is circumstantial fulfilment—that is to say, the Word of God was fulfilled, not because the people concerned knew it, but because in its living efficacy it was itself controlling their actions. Consider John 19:23. The soldiers at the cross of Christ, all unknowingly, fulfilled the Scripture. Did they know the verse which said 'they divide my garments among them, and for my clothing they cast lots' (Ps. 22:18)? But that is exactly what they did!—not because they knew the Bible but because the Bible dominated them. According to custom, they were picking up the 'perks' of the job; but a deeper agency was at work, the Scripture which 'cannot be broken' (John 10:35), the divine Word which 'shall not return to me void, but it shall accomplish what I please, and it shall prosper in the thing for which I sent it' (Isa. 55:11).

Another powerful reference under this heading is Luke 2:1–7. Were we to ask why did Joseph and Mary go up to Bethlehem—and at such an inconvenient time, with Mary's pregnancy almost at full term? The straightforward answer is that Caesar Augustus, in his imperial authority, made a decree that all the world should be taxed. And why did Caesar Augustus make just such a decree at that precise moment? Bible in hand, we answer, because Micah had said that the Messiah must be born in Bethlehem (Micah 5:2). So even Caesar on his throne, all unknowingly, is gripped by the Word of God. It imposes its reality and strength upon the whole world, on its rulers, and any other authorities there may be. The assembled church in Acts 4:27–8 said it all: 'Herod and Pontius Pilate, with the Gentiles and the people of Israel, were gathered together to do whatever your hand and your purpose determined before to be done.'

Proleptic Fulfilment

No, 'proleptic' is not a common word, is it? It means, for example, speaking of something past in the light of what happened to it much later; describing a past occurrence in terms of its future; speaking by hindsight. Thus, we might say, 'her Majesty the Queen was born in 1925,' meaning, 'a little girl was born in 1925 who later became Queen Elizabeth II.' In a word, the coming event casts its shadow before it. That is what 'prolepsis' is.

Others will think differently, but I cannot find a better way of understanding Matthew 2:14–15. Matthew is quoting the words of Hosea, 'Out of Egypt have I called my son' and treating them as prophetic of Jesus' time in Egypt and his subsequent departure out of it. But in Hosea (11:1) the prophet is looking back to Israel's Exodus from Egypt.

In other words, it is a prolepsis. The coming event of Jesus casts its shadow before it in the coming of Israel out of Egypt. It is a foreshadowing of Jesus. This is pretty marvellous and even mind boggling. Why did Israel go down to Egypt and come out of Egypt? Because, in the ultimate, that is what would happen to Jesus. It was because it would happen to him in the future that it happened to them in the past. Their past experience caught the shadow of the coming Messiah, and the Word of God was fulfilled in ways that you would never have thought. Indeed this feature of prolepsis may have been in Matthew's mind throughout his introduction of Jesus. In parallel with Exodus 4:22–3, Jesus is the Son of God in Egypt (Matt. 2:15); in Exodus 14 Israel came to the water (of the Red Sea) and grumbled (vv. 10–12), Jesus came to the Jordan and committed himself to 'fulfilling all righteousness' (Matt. 3:13–17); Israel's record in the wilderness (Exod. 15–17) was one of grumbling and discontent, Jesus in the wilderness (Matt. 4:1–11) met and conquered Satan; in parallel with Exodus 19, Jesus came to the mount (Matt. 5:1), not as another Moses, to act as intermediary, but to sit as God (Exod. 19:18; 20:1) teaching his people his law.

That the pre-history of God's people was thus 'shaped' by the shadow of the Coming One not only enhances the wonder of biblical prophecy but also adorns the dignity and greatness of our Lord Jesus Christ.

Explanatory Fulfilment

This is in some ways very different from other aspects of the theme of fulfilment, but it is a significant element in the linkage between the Testaments. Recall, for example, that we have found it correct, earlier on, to speak of an 'Old Testament enigma'—truths plainly in the Old Testament, left lying, so to speak, on the Old Testament table, but not, at that point, 'making sense', awaiting future—or, as we know, New Testament—clarification. How can Messiah be both 'the mighty God' and also be born as a baby (Isa. 9:6)? How can he be both David's son and David's Lord (Ps. 110:1)? This is what Jesus asked the Pharisees (Luke 20:41–4), not as a trick question but in an attempt to make them face up to what their Bible predicted—the 'messianic enigma of the Old Testament'. Does Isaiah 7:14 mean seriously that Messiah will be born of a virgin? How can he both be 'a root out of a dry ground'—i.e., of earthly origin—and also 'the Arm of the Lord'—God himself come to save (Isa. 53:1–2)? When the New Testament solves these riddles we see 'explanatory fulfilment' at work. The outstanding example of this category of fulfilment is Isaiah 53:9, lit., 'and one appointed with wicked men his grave, and with a rich man (one appointed him to be) in his majestic death.' 'One appointed' is the Hebrew idiom of indefiniteness, equivalent to a passive verb 'his grave was appointed to be'. 'Majestic death' calls attention to the fact that 'deaths' is a 'plural of majesty'. But what about 'wicked men... poor man'? I can well believe that if we were to ask Isaiah what he meant he would have replied, 'I do not know: it just came to me.' And so it stayed, hundreds of years without explanation until Jesus died between two thieves and was buried in the rich man's grave.

Essential Fulfilment

Essential Fulfilment brings us to the final and most important aspect of this link between our Testaments. As a non-gardener I venture here on an illustration, in the hope that it may be botanically correct, but in the knowledge that it perfectly mirrors what happens in our Bibles. Think of a perennial plant, flowering year after year. In its first year it produces the flowers of infancy, perfect in their way yet somewhat pale reflections of the mature flowers of, say, year four. Yet there is a perfect match between the two: the early flowering contains all that the later flowering will display; the later flowering will mirror to perfection what was there in the first year. This is the way the New Testament 'fulfils' the Old.

THE SACRIFICES

Our discussion of the Old Testament sacrifices has already illustrated this sort of fulfilment. We find in the Old Testament the principle of substitution on which the sacrifices were based, the insistence on the perfection of the sacrificial animal, the accomplishment of atonement, the efficacy of the shed blood as the 'beating heart' of the whole system. With our New Testaments in hand, we look back and see, in embryo, what would be the full reality, the perfection of the flowering, in Jesus. The death of Jesus at Calvary did not 'replace' the sacrifices: it brought them to full flower; it completed them; it ended all sacrificial practice by being 'one sacrifice for sins for ever' (Heb. 12:10); it completed, finally, the age-old requirement of substitution through the willing sacrifice of the Son of God. What was there at the start was there, to perfection, at the end.

THE CITY OF GOD

To our Old Testament forebears, the Lord appointed Jerusalem as the city where he had chosen 'to put his name for his habitation', and to be the focal point of their religious observances (Deut. 12:5). The city and its House of the Lord were intended to be at the centre of a world at peace (Deut. 12:10–11); indeed, the building of the house was to mark the end of troubled times and the onset of security and rest (2 Sam. 7:10–11). Since this ideal situation was never realised, it is likely that from early days expectation developed that the true city of God with its attendant blessings was part of Israel's hope, when David's days would return (Isa. 1:26), and even, in some sense, David himself would reign (Ezek. 34:24) But, as expectation developed within the Old Testament, the coming Jerusalem began to outgrow the possibilities of any merely earthly city. It would be integral to the Lord's creation of a new heaven and a new earth (Isa. 65:17–18), the locus of a worldwide gathered people from all the nations, where death would be 'swallowed up', tears no more, and the Lord's salvation the cause of universal, unbroken joy (Isa. 25:6–10a). It would be the goal of the pilgrimage of the ransomed and redeemed (Isa. 35:9–10), coming in singing from the far-flung ends of the earth (Isa. 24:13–16). The Lord himself would reign there (Isa. 24:23), providing the city with its proper name (Ezek. 48:35).

This is the situation the New Testament replicates and develops. It recognises the current Jerusalem 'in bondage with her children'; it recognises also, as a contemporary reality, the 'Jerusalem above', free, the 'mother' of all who are in Christ (Gal. 4:25–6), the city of which we are already citizens (Phil. 3:20), and to which we have already come through the mediation of Jesus, and the power of his blood (Heb. 12:22–4). And, finally, there is the heavenly Jerusalem, the bride of the Lamb, the essential reality of the new creation, the eternal home of those whose names are in the Lamb's book of life (Rev. 21:9–27).

In this biblical review of the theme of the City of God can we fail to see, again, the progress from early flowering to full flower? A truly 'cumulative' progression whereby the embryonic realities of the first, physical, city are still present, but in glorious maturity, in the heavenly city we await, not a 'replacement' but a 'realisation', a perfect 'fulfilment'.

THE PROMISED LAND

We will glance at one last snapshot of Essential Fulfilment: the Lord's promise of a place for his people to possess and live. The promise started with Abram (Gen. 12:1; 13:14–15), and continued throughout the Old Testament period, becoming part of the visionary expectation of the future (e.g., Ezek. 36:24). As with the vision of the city that was yet to be, so, within the Old Testament, the expectation of the land was not static, but developed in ways that make it part of the Old Testament enigma, awaiting the New Testament to explain what is involved. As regards population, not only the promised physical descendants of Abraham but a gathered people from all the nations is yet to assemble. The Messiah will be a 'banner for the nations' (Isa. 11:12). A united, worldwide people will be created (Isa. 19:23–25), and will assemble on the Lord's mountain (Isa. 25:6); the Servant of the Lord will himself be the Lord's salvation 'to the ends of the earth' (Isa. 49:6)—one way of salvation, one God, one people gathered from the 'ends of the earth' and enjoying status as 'the seed (literally) of Israel'—or, in the words of Psalm 87, accorded birth-rights in Zion. In a word, the expectation of the land merges into the expectation of a new heaven and a new earth, the perfect actualisation of the Lord's holy mountain and city (Isa. 2:2–4; 65:17–25; cf., Amos 9:11–15).

When we pass to the New Testament, the expectation of 'the land', a 'place' for the people of God remains unchanged, but it is now, in the very words of our Saviour himself, 'my kingdom' and it is 'not of this world' (John 18:33–6); we join the heroes of faith of old who were 'strangers and pilgrims on the earth', desiring 'a better, that is a heavenly country' (Heb. 11:13–16).

As we seek to grasp this biblical development, it is not that a New Testament concept of 'a kingdom not of this world' replaces the Old Testament geographical land; nor is it a New Testament spiritualisation of what is physical in the Old Testament. No, it is neither a replacement theology nor a spiritualising theology; it is a cumulative theology: the final and perfect flowering, the actualising in full reality of what had always been there.

I will venture another illustration—this time from carpentry. Think of a plank of polished wood. Every element of that polishing shows up what the grain of the wood is like and at every stage along we can say, 'What a beautiful grain there is in this wood.' But when you get to the end of the plank, you can see what carpenters call 'the end grain'—the full demonstration, the full display of the total grain of the wood. It is there at the end, but there is nothing at the end that has not been there all the way along. So Old Testament forms and predictions are the initial polishing of the grain, and the Lord Jesus Christ is the display of the end grain, the full reality of what has always been there. Was anybody ever predicted as was the Lord Jesus? Prediction after prediction after prediction, touching every aspect of his precious earthly life, death, burial, resurrection, ascension and eternal glory. The Lord God is indeed God—the God of unspeakable mercy in that he gave his only Son to be the Lamb of God. The God of unquestionable—indeed, divine—power because from the earliest moment of prediction (Gen. 3:15) and right through the pages of the Old Testament, he was presiding over his creation. He was ordering, controlling and directing history to that very moment when, in the fullness of time (Gal. 4:4), God sent forth his Son, born of a woman, born under the law, to redeem those who were under the law, and to fulfil to the detail what had been forecast. Praise, indeed, be to his great and holy name!

14

SETTLING DOWN TO OUR TASK

I consider myself fortunate in that my education (right up to University entrance) included a sizeable component of memorisation. At a church day school we learned a new hymn by heart every week. Our teachers would not have been impressed by the scorn which classes memory-work as 'parrot learning'. No indeed, memory was (rightly) viewed as a human faculty, and part of the aim of education was to train faculties. Consequently, when I listened to the Bible being read in church services (in those days, quite lengthy 'lessons' from both Testaments at every service), and later when I began personal Bible reading, I found it easy to remember what I heard and read. Memory does not just 'happen'; it needs training and exercise! In more recent years, when it was my privilege to teach Hebrew, people often said 'Oh, I've got such a rotten memory.' But experience made me wonder if there is any such thing as a 'rotten memory.' An untrained memory, possibly; a memory that modern educational methods had allowed to rust? And people who complained of 'a rotten memory' gradually found that they had a memory after all, just waiting to be awakened, and, when exercised, well able to retain the lists of vocabulary and other activities essential to learning a language.

MEMORY

All this applies to Bible knowledge. If we want to retain what we hear—not in one ear and out the other, but stopping half way and staying there; if we want to retain through the day what we read in the morning, there is no short cut. It takes memory; it means resurrecting our memories; and this means putting them to work. It means committing something to memory every day—a phrase, a verse, a few verses—whatever. A good idea is to jot down the chosen verse in a notebook so that it is available for refreshment and revision—and, of course, each of us must choose what version of the Bible we find most easily memorable: it is giving my age away to say that to me nothing is more easily committed to memory than the King James Bible—or, nowadays, the New King James. But, suit yourself. The essential thing is to blow the dust off your memory and get it in working order.

THE BIBLE EVERY YEAR

The almost invariable response to the suggestion of reading through the Bible every year is 'Oh, I don't think I could manage that!'—and, to be frank, it does sound daunting. Look at it this way, however; my copy of NKJV runs to 1217 pages. Is it too much to read just over three pages a day? If you buy a daily paper you read far, far more than that! I like to break down the three pages into four daily readings. First of all, I suggest it is important that we always include in our daily diet, something from the four Gospels. In this way we are constantly refreshing our portrait of Jesus. Less than half a page a day gets us through the Gospels in a year, the same applies to the remainder of the New Testament. Just over half a page guarantees covering Isaiah to Malachi—and now that you have grasped the idea you can do the mathematics for your own Bible. In my Bible, Psalms runs to 160 columns of print—far less than one column a day for a year's reading! You can break the material down in whatever way suits your own daily pattern of morning and evening readings, or your 'elevenses' dip into the Bible. All you need to do is keep a record of what you have read.

PROJECTS

Remember this is Bible Reading, not Bible Study. Its sole purpose is to build up an ever deepening layer of knowledge of what the Bible contains. But, without losing sight of this great purpose, your reading can impinge on study in this very simple way: when you are reading Psalms, for example, you could have a 'project', to collect what the Psalms teach about prayer, or the titles they use for the Lord; reading the Gospels you might collect information on how Jesus related to people, or what he taught about his reasons for coming into the world. Or if you are reading a book of the Bible with which you are not too familiar, it is good to write the briefest summary as you go on—only don't let anything become complicated!

FLEXIBILITY

One of the great advantages of this way of reading though the Bible is its flexibility. If your early mornings are a frantic rush, a little adjustment can still rescue ten minutes with your Bible—and if you need a special motivation to do this, read Isaiah 50:4, predicting Jesus, the Servant of the Lord, and compare it with Mark 1:35. It's such a simple way in which we can model ourselves on him. If, like me, you have reached the blessed ranks of the retired, the early morning is a great time for leisurely and prolonged reading. Be practical, be businesslike, be realistic. The Bible is the precious Word of God: our greatest, most privileged possession.

GET REAL

A friend of mine has recently returned from Central Africa where she was teaching English and Theology to a class of undergraduates who were also ministers in training. She managed to secure a supply of Bibles for them to use as text books during the course, distributing them before each session, and carefully collecting them in after each class. At the end of the course, she said, 'Now write your names in your Bibles: they are yours'— and she watched grown men break down in tears (first of disbelief, then of overwhelming joy) because at last they had their own Bibles.

'Teach us to love your sacred Word
And view our Saviour there!'

AFTERWORD

D. A. Carson

Alec Motyer is one of the people I wish I knew better than I do. But I suspect I know some things about him better than he thinks I do.

When I first went to England in 1972 to begin research at Cambridge University, Alec Motyer was a name buzzing around CICCU (– Cambridge Inter-Collegiate Christian Union—for American readers, the Cambridge chapter of IVCF). Every Spring, CICCU devotes six Saturday evening 'Bible Readings' to one speaker and one extended passage of Scripture. The previous year they had asked Alec, so on six consecutive Saturday evenings he came up to Cambridge from Bristol, where he served in a theological college, to expound Isaiah. Reports universally affirmed that these expositions were masterful, and sometimes irrepressibly funny. I secured a copy of the tapes, primarily because CDs and MP3s had not yet been invented. Alec began his first address by saying, in effect, that while he was grateful for the privilege of expounding Isaiah in six sessions, nevertheless, owing to the paucity of the material, he thought he would throw in Jeremiah as well. He then spent the next hour leading his hearers carefully and thoughtfully through Isaiah 1–12.

In those addresses (including this opening gambit) one could read much of Alec's life, nicely summed up: a Christian theologian who loves the Old Testament, delights in expository preaching, is especially devoted to the prophecy of Isaiah, constantly reflects on the trajectories that link the Old and New Testaments and draw people to Jesus—and over all of it a wonderful combination of serious reverence, pastoral application, and impish Irish humour.

Alec's son Stephen was an undergraduate at Cambridge during my early years there, and more than once Stephen invited me to his room for coffee with his father when Alec came to visit his son. Probably neither of them remember those discussions, but I do. The combination of theological and cultural insight, the utter freedom from pretension, the marriage of confessional orthodoxy and charming wit, the personal relationships—it was all very captivating.

Through various channels I followed Alec's ministry from afar, not least his move to church ministry in Bournemouth. More than once I have spoken at conferences where he had preached two or three years earlier, and always those who had heard him were filled with gratitude to God for his ministry. By this time I was of course resolved to read everything he wrote. Over the years came a steady flow of valuable books and articles. These include at least four books on Isaiah, including the latest, *Isaiah by the Day*, which is simultaneously a fresh translation and robust devotional notes that take the serious lay reader right through the prophecy. His commitment to Old Testament theology has produced another string of books. His reflections on how the New Testament cites the Old surface in several others, the most seminal of which is his *Look to the Rock: An Old Testament Background to Our Understanding of Christ*. Today there are many books that treat this complex subject, pitched at various levels and operating with highly diverse presuppositions. But when Alec published *Look to the Rock*, it was not only ground-breaking but seminal—or, more accurately, it was thoughtfully recovering what is sometimes called 'whole Bible' biblical theology that was frequently lost to view in the twentieth century, and opening the eyes of Alec's readers to what had been lost.

Alec's pastoral commitments surface most strongly in his popular expositions and thematic studies on James, Philippians, Amos, Exodus, and 1 & 2 Thessalonians. They also show up compellingly in *Life 2: The Sequel– What Happens When You Die*. His denominational convictions appear in his work on infant baptism. His primer on preaching, *Preaching? Simple Teaching on Simply Preaching*, is one of the best there is, displaying the work of a master who knows his subject so well he can make it look 'simpler' than it is, and therefore less daunting.

So it is a huge privilege to commend the author of the Pocket Guide you now hold in your hand—although, quite frankly, his work speaks for itself so well that it does not need me to approve it. But I still wish I knew Alec better than I do.